Psychodynamic Running

The Complete, Definitive,
Madman's Guide
to Distance Running
and the Marathon

Ethan Gologor

SelectBooks, Inc.
(New York)

Psychodynamic Running: The Complete, Definitive, Madman's Guide to Distance Running and the Marathon
©2007 Ethan Gologor

This edition published by SelectBooks, Inc. For information address SelectBooks, Inc., One Union Square West, New York, New York 10003

First Edition

Library of Congress Cataloging-in-Publication Data

Gologor, Ethan.

Psychodynamic running : the complete, definitive, madman's guide to distance running and the marathon / Ethan Gologor. – 1st ed.

p. cm.

Includes index.

ISBN-13: 978-1-59079-110-3 (pbk. : alk. paper)

ISBN-10: 1-59079-110-X

1. Marathon running–Psychological aspects. I. Title.

GV1065.G65 2007
796.42'52–dc22

2007002456

Manufactured in the United States of America

10 9 8 7 6 5 4 3 2 1

To Matt and Ben, all grown up, much too fast, but ever "the kids."

Contents

Acknowledgments
My Cup Runneth Over

It will be obvious from my first paragraph that this book is primarily dedicated to my running partners ("Drop your hands ... take longer breaths ... drink!"), my running therapists, my running strategists, my running nutritionists, my running couturiers, my running rabbis, my kids, Matthew and Benjamin. It should also be obvious that—unlike tennis but like sex—running is something you can do alone, but there's something to be said for trying it alongside somebody else.

Thanks to Vicki for teaching me that there are truly crazy people who get out there seven days a week, fifty-two weeks a year before 7 a.m. to join the birds, the dog walkers, and the stumblers wending their way home after a late-night binge, but you don't have to be like them. Thanks to Jerry, even as he was amazed at the idea that I was going to do the Big One, for instructing me about bending and shortening strides on hills. Thanks to Roger and Joel and Walter for listening to the woes of the body and mind associated with this activity while continuing to remind me that there were always tennis balls to hit. Thanks to Bari for offering the biggest cheers on and between First and Fifth Avenues, and for trying against all odds to provide some technical support to someone who has a better chance of deciphering his illegible notes than figuring out how to format a floppy or burn a disc. Thanks to Shari for joining in the cheering when she'd hardly learned my name; and to Terry, even as she was teaching me the location of all the organs and body parts that I could expect to damage, for reminding me I might still have an ounce of youth to exude when all else seemed drained. Thanks to Pauline and Fayetta, who encouraged the Walking Group at the College, thereby giving some unofficial okay to my disappearing during some office hours to train and do my "research," and to the others at Medgar: Pat and Ed and Frances and Hiroko and members of the "Psyching Team," who, *inter alia,* gave support at all watering holes; Greg and Areen, for decoding statistics masquerading as hieroglyphics; President Edison O. Jackson, both for his encouragement of the project from its first baby steps, and for proving daily that having stentorian, homiletic tendencies does not prevent your walking the walk as well as talking the talk; Mike Fitzgerald for being there at the last minute (the last couple of hours, actually) to prevent whatever there is from vanishing forever into cyberspace, and to Leonid for backing him up and backing the files up, since everything these days is backed up and apparently needs to be backed up; and Rhonda, for cleaning up so many housekeeping and mousekeeping details. Thanks to Mijanou Spurdle and Bob Weiner, whose experience measuring pie charts and net posts, respectively, is so unparalleled that it somehow extrapolates easily to measuring the significance of every step of every race they've taken. Thanks to Amy, who not only knows everything from advertising to zinc bars and touches everyone's soul from Hell's Angels to Hunter Thompson, but whose talent for tattooing the pragmatic onto the fantastic with dramatic, if not Socratic, irony is unique. Thanks to Penny, even if she couldn't re-arrange my positive and negative imagery, for diverting my concern with bleeding from the course to the cover. Thanks to Emily, whose insights and footnotes kickbox their way across the finish line while you're still hunched over the start retying the shoelaces on yours. And thanks to all those strangers from Bay Ridge to Williamsburg, from Greenpoint to First Avenue, from Harlem to Central Park, who offered everything from popsicles to donuts to paper towels, none of which I managed to get a tight hold on, but whose dexterity, compared to that of one aging novice runner they were trying to assist, was hardly the problem.

I think especially of all the prognosticators of doom, repeat-edly telling me I didn't need to do this, that there are so many other healthy forms of exercise, even cardio-stuff that doesn't damage your knees, for they too were well-wishers simply cov-ering their bets. Yes, to them and the others not so directly pessimistic (like those who would coyly ask me what time I was aiming for, to which I'd always reply "December"), I give thanks for midwifing a most unlikely prospect to give birth to this pair of unlikely twins: a marathon run and a book to try to tell it like it was and is and might be.

1

Introduction: Psychologist, Run Thyself

*

At precisely 10:00 a.m. on November 6th, 2005, after I'd made my rounds among the 37,000 runners lounging or pacing about at Fort Wadsworth in Staten Island, I stripped off the medical badge that I'd worn the last three years while running (operating, being in charge of) the "Psyching Team," replaced it with number 46,645, and headed for the starting line. This was to be the start of the last leg, or the last 138,435 legs, of a journey I'd begun some six years earlier (without quite knowing it), some two-and-a-half years earlier (without quite understanding it), and some twenty weeks earlier (with a creeping awareness of what I was really letting myself in for): the Marathon Madness Journey.

To be sure, in this day and age where triathletes and triathlons and Iron Man competitions regularly occupy the athletic landscape and wedge neologisms into our vocabulary almost daily; where wheelchairs and crutches and amputees can be found regularly on many a racecourse; where runners are not only used to advertise sneakers and sports drinks but show up in stockbroker ads, on bus stop kiosks, and on the cover of Introductory Psychology textbooks; where everyone I run into (encounter) in the supermarket or synagogue or classroom has either been doing it for years or is married to someone who has or else has sworn it off after doing it for years; where everything from the arduous and endless baseball season playoffs to sixteen hours of Comedy Central's *Blue-Collar* stand-up routines to "Movies-You'll-Thank-Us-For" on the American Movie Channel to Howard Stern's New Year's Eve Show to five-set tennis matches to the Live 8 concerts are referred to as "marathons," running one appears not to be the singular accomplishment that it was a generation ago. But for me, need I say, it was. Runners may be all over the place—new runners, old runners, athletic runners, nonathletic runners—all with their stories, but the marathon course (or any race-course, for that matter) wasn't exactly a milieu into which I readily fit. At some point in this odyssey, in fact, I felt it necessary to remind myself—just in case I needed incontrovertible support for what I wanted to do, which was quit—of all the characteristics or conditions I thought conducive to running, and the ways in which I fell short of meeting them:

1) I don't live in the hills of Colorado where the morning sun bathes the eucalyptus leaves in a shimmering array of rainbow colors and the evening sun reflects the cactus sprigs along the piebald path as your footsteps echo the egrets' ambling with their young to the nests in the bushes beneath the ospreys cooing in the branches above and the runner can't help feeling one with the universe. I am an angry New Yorker, living in the densest neighborhood outside of Hong Kong, in a modest Manhattan apartment dwelling with hundreds of anonymous others who each morning scurry silently into the

elevator, spilling their coffee over my sneakers and path to the lobby door which, as I hurriedly exit in an effort to start running, leads to one's super's hose and two dog leashes which I must hurdle, three double strollers I must skirt, four hidden driveways I must approach very cautiously, five delivery men with hand trucks around which I must detour, six sauntering sidewalk-hogging couples, seven cell-phone sidewalk dawdlers, eight furniture stores with sidewalk showrooms, nine maids a milking ... and all this before I get to the first intersection where ten cabs a-turning, eleven cars a-honking, twelve delivery-boy-bicycles blocking ... on to the river walkway where dozens of skateboarders, roller bladers and skip-roping schoolkids are making it very difficult to begin, much less continue, a modest two-mile run. Yes, I know there are plenty of urban runners, but most of them must be tourists or migrants from the Midwest who do not have my own form of carefully nurtured, fifty-year-old road rage that manages to be suppressed, though not very successfully, on escalators (must they stand two-abreast and block we who are trying to get somewhere!?), ATM lines (must they re-count their money, pocket it, and examine their receipt before they move to the side?), and supermarket cashier lines—especially so-called express ones—where the $1.79 total for my predecessor is going to be paid for either with a credit card ("Cash? People still carry cash?") or else 29 or 54 or 79 very deliberately counted pennies. No, I do not need a new activity to help nudge me into the institution or straitjacket or police blotter for which I've been evidently long preparing.

2) I have been a tennis player most of my life. I enjoy tennis. I've written about tennis. I've played in tournaments, and actually won a few. I've taught a course in Sport Psychology. I watch all kinds of sports. My kids are athletic and we play tennis together, not just on Father's Day but on other days as well, and many of my friends and acquaintances I've first met at the

tennis court. I don't need another form of exercise, whatever the vital differences between aerobic and anaerobic forms, thank you.

3) I don't drink much water. As a tennis player I found, or thought I did, that even in 100-degree weather, when my opponents and partners were bringing huge jugs with them, I took a few sips before playing and that was enough. More than that, particularly at every changeover, made me sluggish. If running requires the constant hydrating that all seem to advocate, it's not for me.

4) I've been known to drink other stuff. Not just a glass or two of white wine at dinner. Hard liquor. With a degree of regularity. To the chagrin of many. Also many cups of tea. Maybe that's what hydrates me. They say that both dehydrate you, but I don't know. The wisdom on the subject of hydration seems to change as regularly as knowledge about running shoes and pronation, whatever that is. Water intoxication, often referred to as "hyponatremia" and a serious danger for runners, was nearly unknown a decade ago. It doesn't even appear in the glossary of marathon books written not too long ago.[1] But articles on the topic now appear with stunning regularity in the *New York Times*. Even that well-known dehydrator caffeine is not, according to the latest information, a dehydrator at all. But regardless, I don't imagine that this imbibing, even if it forms a good part of the life pattern of some well-known long distance writers, is the best preparation for the long-distance runner.

5) I don't get enough sleep. I don't get any sleep. I've been known to wake up six times during the night. Get plenty of rest if you want to be a runner, particularly a marathoner? Tell it to my prostate.

---

1 G. Kislevitz. *First Marathons.* Halcottsville, New York: Breakaway Books; 2003.

6) I'm Jewish. I'm too Jewish. You want to know the difference between a Jewish and a Gentile runner? The Gentile stands tall at the starting line, head held high, looking forward to the experience, sharing with all others what time he hopes to achieve, pointing out what a beautiful day it is for a run (80 degrees?—"Nice and sunny;" 20 degrees?—"Nice and brisk;" 30 mph winds?—"Will keep you cool;" Torrential downpour?—"Will keep you cool") and wishing everyone well. The Jewish runner talks to no one except his wife or girlfriend on the sideline, asking if she has another power gel (he only has two), how many port-a-potties there are going to be along the way, worrying if that ache in his calf muscle that he experienced two hours ago upon awakening is about to resurface, while three times retying his shoelaces, which he knows are not long enough to stay tied but just long enough to trip over, taking off his shoes repeatedly in a vain effort to prevent his socks from bunching up, hiking up his shorts which are too wide and already chafing in the groin, hitting himself over the head for not having enough Vaseline to rub on his other chafable parts, and listening to the portable weather station in his ear or on his wrist to get the latest update on temperature, humidity, and barometric pressure so he can be sure that he's taken entirely the wrong wardrobe. In addition, he tells no one about his plans, certainly not what time he hopes to attain, not even that he hopes to finish, because that will prove a jinx, a curse, *kinehurra* (the evil eye shouldn't get me). He doesn't assume anything good will ever just happen. He has no faith in accounts receivable. If I am about to receive $80 from the copayments of some patients later in the afternoon and I could use the cash, I go to the bank earlier and withdraw $80 because you never know … it might be closed, each patient might forget or say he forgot, there might be a transit strike. Make the assumption that things will turn out as they should and the gods will humble you for your arrogance.

Make the assumption that you will win the race and the gods will punish you for having "too swell a head." You can compliment someone to his face, but very moderately, lest he become too full of himself. We are responsible for promoting each other's humility, not our chest thumping. Reserve your best accolades for when he's not around. Yes, says the Talmud, "If I am not for me who will be?" but on the other hand, "If I am only for me, what am I?" Yes, says Buber, you should always remember "For my sake the world was created," but also, "I am nothing but dust and ashes." Now are these "other hands" going to be applauding your confidence in an immense undertaking? Or, if you dare tell people what time (even with some latitude) you think you'll pass certain spots on the marathon route, will they be covering their faces in humiliation when you don't show up? So keep it to yourself. You can inflict your own humiliation quite well, thank you.

7) I am not methodical. While I've been known to exercise some discipline, and at times even great discipline (you don't just toss off school dissertations), I tend to work in spurts. Having an idea for an article or research project, I don't work on it a little at a time and finish it according to schedule. Instead I seem to build up a head of steam and hope it buoys me on high before it evaporates or suffocates me. So how could I even contemplate the routine buildup that must be, as I've learned, a marathoner's *sine qua non?* Twenty weeks before? Five times a week? Build up to 20, then 25, then 30 miles? Please. Who has the time for any of this?

8) Running, as I've been at pains to indicate, is totally new to me. And I am not particularly curious about new things. I don't want to be told about new diets or routines that will require some adjustment (running has a few). I don't even like listening to people except in therapy, when I'm the designated listener. I did take a course or two once, and had inspiring teachers, but

that was a while ago. I had also, in my youth, traveled the world and expressed some interest in other cultures and practices, but enough was enough. Now I know everything, so don't try to change me. If you start telling me I need to have my foot examined (as well as my head) in order to secure the right running shoe, I will remind you that I have sneakers (all right, tennis shoes) that are older than you are and that they serve me quite well. And that's my newest pair. I've got another that may be a bit worn on the sides, but they're canvas and have polyurethane soles so they're more flexible and never get holes and I alternate them with the other. So I don't want to think about thermalayer turtlenecks or mesh pants or power-dry fleece trainers because I wouldn't know what to think about them.

9) I don't go to doctors; and if I go, I don't listen to them; and if I listen to them, I forget their advice and lose their prescriptions. No, I'm not a self-destructive self-abuser, despite what some of my ex-wives and girlfriends might insist, but I don't take stress tests nor even roughly measure my calorie intake nor know the difference between saturated and unsaturated fats, and am lucky if I consume the FDA's recommended daily allotment of fruits and vegetables in a week—maybe two.

10) I'm too old. Did I say that already? I know, I know, the stories abound about the woman who did her first marathon at 72, or the 80 year-olds who run it in three hours, and there was probably a 95 year-old signed up for the one I was to do, but these are all flexible, lean, positive-thinking, yoga-and-yogurt-and-brown-rice paragons of health who, because of all their other wonderful positive attributes, will outlive Methuselah. I tried Pilates and tai-chi once each when someone recommended them for building up the "core," and not only couldn't I bend my legs nearly enough to get them anywhere near the angles required, I couldn't even understand

the instruction about where they were supposed to end up facing. I was like a learning-disabled third-grader who couldn't
tell the teacher's left from right, much less alternate his movements from clockwise to counterclockwise while singing "You
put your left leg in and you turn it all about ..." And when I
took a moderate stretching class once, as soon as the instruc-
tor came by my mat to give me—literally—a little extra push,
I cramped immediately in the opposing muscle. Twice. It was
apparent that 100 years of tennis playing, even for three or
four hours in 95-degree weather, had done nothing to facilitate any other physical faculties of mine. Something about aer-
obics and anaerobics. A fish out of water doesn't swim. Or fly
like an egret. Or occupy the same universe with which he's
supposed to feel at one.

So now that I was able to summarize all the personal and
cosmic forces operating against me, I was reminded of British
philosopher Herbert Spenser, who once advocated following
this procedure whenever you had a choice to make: First make
a detailed list of all the reasons for and against one of the
options, then assign a numerical weight to each of these reasons, then total the columns and whichever came out ahead,
do the opposite. Had I been "protest(ing) too much?" You
could have fooled me, for it wasn't until I had stood alone in
my orange "corral" at Fort Wadsworth for an hour, awaiting
the opening gun, silently hoping that sometime before the
end of the week I would somehow find my way to the finish
line, that I came to see, misfit or no, why the whole thing did
seem suddenly to make a perverse kind of sense.

My kids, no longer aged five and eight, having learned all I
could teach them about negotiating New York streets amongst
the errant garbage trucks, taxis, and bicyclists,[2] who have run

---

2 Lessons that eventually landed us in front of the Taxi Commission and
   on the Op-Ed page of the *Times*: E. Gologor. "Crashing Red Lights." *New
   York Times:* July 23, 1981; p. A23.

six marathons between them, had succeeded, despite my sincere and earnest protests, in passing me their baton. They'd been trying to teach me about pronation. And electrolytes. And fartleks. My academic colleagues, having investigated just about everything sport psychologists could think of without getting up from their chairs—distinguishing, *inter alia,* situational motivation from the somehow quite different extrinsic motivation, and integrated regulation from introjected regulation, and mindfulness from acceptance from commitment— were hovering more over statistical tables than the water tables that line most courses (at which my psyching team regularly volunteers, and which could use a few more Ph.Ds). And finally, my unconscious, growing no older than the rest of me but becoming much more cognizant of the date looming for the past 35 years in the corner of my quarterly pension-fund statements (in fact, it was due to arrive exactly seven weeks after the marathon), apparently needed to make its own statement. Was that classroom door that I exited last semester going to lock forever behind me and in an instant, as in *About Schmidt,* blow into dust all traces of my erstwhile presence? Was I going to slip quietly into the retirement night? Was that armchair on which I tuned in to my patients' dramas going to transform itself unnoticeably and unceremoniously into a rocking chair? Come on now, doctor: Medicare or Marathon?

So it was fitting. As well as unfitting. Because just over two years earlier, despite having demonstrated some of that speed and facility on the tennis court for most of my life, the very thought of running made me wince with pain. Not only was I inept at it, I couldn't conceive, for all those reasons listed, of that situation ever changing. A few yards to catch a bus or traffic light, and I was panting. Maybe I had done a mile in college gym class a few centuries ago but, with one exception, surely nothing much like it since. Until my kids decided to take it up to balance those eight hours they were spending behind desks in their first postcollege jobs, I had stared in amazement at all those trendy joggers circling the reservoir or Central Park's Upper and Lower Loops, as I came to learn they were called. Why are they doing this? This is not a sport. This is masochism. And actually, I only joined and later became captain of this marathon psyching team so I would have a chance of catching my offspring, perhaps literally, at the finish line. Despite some background in the popular and growing field of Sport Psychology, despite my reservations that this group of clinicians (as well as the academics) was a hybrid bunch of frustrated gym rats sublimating their over-the-hill Olympic fantasies into dreams of becoming coaches to the stars, I was even more skeptical what we psychologists could do for runners. Help them to think positively? To visualize the finish line? To absorb the crowd's energy? All perhaps well-documented appurtenances of the pretentiously scientific social sciences, but these kernels of psychological wisdom will get you through 26.2 miles? Forgive me my skepticism.

A Bit of a Backstory

On January 1st, 1999, my son Matthew made one New Year's resolution: He was going to run the New York Marathon. Despite having only recently started running, despite getting sufficient exercise as a regular and somewhat accomplished tennis player, despite having a full-time teaching job which often required late-night and weekend hours, he was going to run. Okay, I said, but I regretted that he probably wouldn't be able to expect much help from me. First of all, I can't do it. Second, I don't particularly find any appeal in it. Third, I know little about it. And fourth, I must be on record somewhere as having dismissed it, along with bike riding and horseback riding, as maybe a healthy form of exercise but certainly not a sport, and (in typical psychological fashion) added that it was to sport as masturbation was to sex. He was fine, he said; he didn't need my help, and in fact, may have been pleased that this was going to be exclusively his thing. And it wasn't as if he hadn't proven he was a pretty good and diverse athlete, having played on the rugby team at Oberlin (the only college, I believe, to have matched Columbia University's football losing streak, which lasted over seven years), but his is a broad-shouldered, mesomorphic body (these apparently still exist, as fitness expert Tamilee Webb has designed different programs for each, depending on your various body-part ratios), and if you'll notice, my broad-hipped women friends forever tell me, all those cute runners are ectomorphic types.[3]

Months later, it's true, I was called on to hold those water bottles and power gels in the pouring rain, sheltered by only a partial overhang next to the Central Park reservoir, as he did nine laps (essentially a half-marathon). But by that time in his training he could have used all the help anyone could offer and, despite my reservations and aversion, I had to sympathize with and assist his effort. And while on the Big Day he was to end up crashing into the all-too-familiar 21-mile "wall" and hobbling somewhat deliriously through those last few miles— thereby deferring his "family reunion" by an interminable 90 minutes while I paced up and down, waiting for him to be let out of the medical tent—he had accomplished his goal and then some. This guy who'd never run more than a couple of miles in his life had, with less than a year's practice, run a marathon in under four hours. And it changed his life.

For one thing, if not quite like Forrest Gump, he kept moving. He decided to take a trip around the world. Literally. Alone. A *tour du monde*, as the travel agent proudly emphasized.

---

3 T. Webb. *Workouts for Dummies*. New York: Hungry Minds; 1998.

New York to Germany to South Africa to Dubai to Mumbai to Katmandu to Bangkok to San Francisco. He started beating me in chess. He began dating exceptional young women. He grew a foot-and-a-half. Where he'd been modest and retiring before, he was now confident and aggressive. He asked questions. He said "no" to people. He cracked jokes. He took a brief course in stand-up comedy and got up repeatedly in front of strangers to make them laugh or make a fool of himself. And he decided to do it again. The New York Marathon, that is.

And this time his kid brother joined him. He who lying in his crib had been described by one of my athletic friends as indeed having "a runner's body," but who also had put his athletic prowess into other sports, was going to put it to the test. They trained together, pushing each other as only competitive but amicable brothers can. And now, on their loops around Central Park, I was brought into action again. As they did run the arcs, so did I cut the chords. And to those eyebrow-raising acquaintances, skeptical that all this togetherness meant I hadn't cut the umbilical ones (cords, that is), I raised my bottle in an ironic toast. I was the water boy. The dry-shirt boy. The strawberry-banana power-gel boy. And for two consecutive Novembers I did indeed grab them at the finish line, after the "walls" and the cramps and the overly hot temperatures, as they finished within minutes of each other.

In late 2003, when little brother Benjamin, with equally little experience or previous inclination, had completed his second and Matthew his third marathon, Benjy, quite out of the blue, informed me that despite the difficulties of getting into the race, I could become eligible to run it in 2005 by becoming a member of the New York Road Runners and completing nine races in 2004. This marathon would occur just prior to what I've indicated I was trying to avoid thinking about, my Medicare birthday. He now denies, by the way, modestly refusing to take any credit, that he said any such thing.

And so the craziest of ideas had been planted. And while I was looking elsewhere, cultivating a few more familiar gardens, it was fed some sunlight and water. And snow and wind and Gatorade. And somehow, despite all that well-founded, cultivated resistance, it started to take root, proving that insanity is hereditary. You catch it from your children.

Before I knew it, I was paying some attention to the world of runners. I learned that I wasn't supposed to run in those sneakers, even my "newer" pair, because they weren't "running shoes." I was taught on which end of a treadmill to stand (strictly by chance, I guessed in which direction to face). I became knowledgeable, if not expert, on "Coolmax" (clothing) and "Gu" (food) and in a few months, dare I say, I doubled my lifetime output. I could actually run two miles. Not without cost, mind you. I've run through (endured) a gamut of injuries, literally, from head (dizzy) to toe (blackened). Parts of the body I didn't know existed entered my vocabulary as they got strained *(iliotibial band)* or inflamed *(plantar fasciitis)*. More familiar parts started secreting fluids of different hues than they used to (yes, aged male runners, that prostate insists on getting into the act).

And of course it is now with a great deal of astonishment and gratitude that I thank both my kids for holding my hands as they pushed me toward that starting line on what I never in my wildest or soberest of moments would have contemplated. Matthew escorted me around my first five-mile loop in preparation for that first four-mile race of 2004, when a month earlier I couldn't complete a lap of the reservoir (1.55 miles). Benjy joined me on that and a couple of other races, particularly the Brooklyn Half-Marathon, having coached me and served, along with his girlfriend Bari, as my oasis the previous week when I ran my first ten miles in hilly Prospect Park. In the next year-and-a-half, Matthew did a few speed-work (slow speed-work, that is) exercises with me, ran with me for the last seven miles of my first 20-mile practice run, and took me across the Queensboro Bridge a week before the event to familiarize myself with the terrain—the very inclined terrain, that is. Benjy recommended I do the "ten-mile to the finish" group run two weeks before the event, and joined me on a few other training stints around the park, including waiting a couple of endless hours with Bari as I struggled to complete my first twelve-miler in the park. Along the way, I was to become familiar, through their agency, not only with cool max and Gu, but the catalogue of Gatorades ("Endurance," "Recovery," and whatnot) and running bibles, including the *Marathon Training for Dummies* (no argument there) to *First Marathons* run by people even up to the age of 51.[4,5]

The last and most extraordinary preparatory leg consisted of the twenty weeks between Father's Day and the event, when I somehow summoned the discipline to stick to a regular, if not rigorous, running schedule despite every temptation and distraction and rationalization to give it up. (When I complained daily to a friend about my pains and how little confidence I had, she would "comfort" me by suggesting "maybe it's not your sport.") And I know that this period, while now pretty much a blur, is what did it for me. On that Father's Day, the kids and I ran the six-mile loop together. They said I was breathing a little better, I allowed myself the first glimmer of confidence that it might actually happen, and we then scurried off to the tennis courts where traditionally we had spent part of this day, and I could actually gain a sense of pleasure from doing something physical.

And speaking of blurs, the actual run, as I recall it some weeks later, is mostly a mélange of dozens of sharp and gradual turns; of two million spectators, all seeming to be either

---

4   T. Drenth. *Marathon Training for Dummies.* New York: John Wiley & Sons; 2003.

5   G. Kislevitz. *First Marathons.* Halcottsville, New York: Breakaway Books; 2003.

blowing cacophonous trumpets or extending generous high-fives; of 37,516 runners' heels (was I behind all of them?); of too many bridges and not enough bathrooms; of tiny kids in skullcaps handing out water in Williamsburg while their Chasidic fathers, in broad-brimmed fur-lined hats, turned away with a "what-is-this madness?" shrug; of spilled cups and (new this year?) big yellow Sponge-Bob water things littering the ground toward the 19th mile up First Avenue; and of hundreds of runners stumbling or walking through the Bronx and Harlem and Fifth Avenue as the 70-degree heat and 90 percent humidity was beginning to take its toll.

But what is not a blur (and the significance of this phenomenon I hope to highlight in the chapter on social facilitation) was Matthew (and friend Shari who somehow was dragged into this familial madness), at mile 6 and 14 and 19 and 21 with a big smile, a sign exhorting "Go, go Ethan", and a camera, the framed product of which now sits above my desk, and Benjy, hands filled with bananas and water and gels, asking me at mile 18 what I needed and then joining me to run miles 23 to 25 before they kicked him off the course. And there was Bari who, having been through this spectator ordeal three previous years and who had expressed herself worriedly, "Oh no you're not really going to … I don't know if I can handle another anxiety-filled few months of this," was now somehow cheering louder than anyone on the route. And there was everyone else I knew catching me (my unofficial advisor, intermittent social worker, and experienced runner, Vicki, cleared a path for me at water stations from miles 19 to 23 and kept telling me, with apparently no less astonishment than I was expressing, that I really was "looking good"), if not in the actual race, then at the family reunion or after-party (which lasted nearly a week).

Am I going to do it again? Now that I've actually completed a marathon, I have become more aware of the many post-marathon oaths never to run one again, sworn to by individuals who then complete another half dozen or 50. This will not be me. I have finished running my marathon. I have finished running marathons. I had, apparently, something to prove, however complex or simpleminded. I am quite happy with not having to prove it again.

I have not gotten the "bug" or even a modest high. My friend Lorrie, who ran four of them, believes it a myth—maybe like the vaginal orgasm (What's the latest on that? Are there different runners' highs?)—and like me is apt, whenever anyone brings it up, to speak of runner's lows, since we've had plenty of them.

But a "high" was no more the objective than fun. Is that not the addict's downfall? To believe that the quick fix, the substance-induced euphoria, supplants the longer, more sustained satisfaction that comes from a deep commitment to something that takes years to accomplish? Not for nothing do people talk of running as an addiction (sport psychologists have tried to distinguish good addictions from bad, and I'm not sure how successful they've been, but more on this later). Work is what it was, work disguised as sport, a realization that makes sport more than play, a theme I'll take up in the next chapter.

Did I feel afterward, as others so often seem to proclaim, that I could do anything? No, it hasn't changed my life dramatically, as I think it did Matthew's, but I'm a bit more set in my ways than he. I will probably not institute a program to put an end to global terrorism. Or reduce global warming. Or win Wimbledon. Or become C.E.O. of Google. After I win the Oscar for the title role in *Richard III*. When Jessica Simpson and Jennifer Love Hewitt (are those their names?) will fall in love with me.

No, what I did feel after crossing that finish line was not euphoric and was very slow in coming. And I'm still not quite sure of it. An accomplishment, to be sure. Perhaps a major one.

But I found myself looking ahead as soon as I crossed the finishing line. Where is the family reunion? Where is the water? How soon for a beer? When you finish something, perhaps even writing a book, you may understandably want to hunt for the celebration, but it's natural also not quite to believe it. Am I really finished? Are we ever quite finished? Maybe that's why others are determined to do it again. So they won't be finished. Was I happy to get my certificate days later, suitable for framing, of marathon completion from the Road Runners along with their letter of congratulation? Sure, but why was my net time (eight minutes faster than clock time), my real time, not displayed first? And all those split times, calculated not by my chip but by the similarly eight-minute-too-slow clock time, did not do justice to my run.

In the days that followed, was I removed from petulance or even anger now that I'd achieved the milestone? Hardly. I still feel the anger at patients who don't show or don't call. Maybe more so. And frankly, when I stare at the clutter of papers flowing in every direction on my desk, table, and even bed, I experience a familiar now-how-the-hell-am-I-ever-going-to-fight-my-way-out-of-this feeling. It is still difficult to roll out of bed in the morning. And despite all my dietary improvements the previous weeks (kale, flax, omega-3s and -8s, as if I knew what these things were), those cookies and double chocolate ice cream packages started looking good. I haven't quite regained all of those eight pounds I'd lost in training, but I can only hope, aside from the photos and certificate of completion, that I won't be hard put pretty soon to prove I've done it. I shall also feel, should I ever finish this account, a sense of accomplishment, but not that I am Superman.

Did it all sort itself out later when I settled down to some modest exercise? No, when I digested a bit more completely what I'd done and started running again, nothing was terribly different from the way it had been earlier, particularly when running. Or so I at first thought. And that is a big part of what all this did for me. It got me thinking.

So when I went out to the park exactly a week later, even duplicating the 10:22 a.m. starting time that I'd taken off at, to see if I could move a modest three miles, and did so with only a couple of pains and measuring only a few seconds-per-mile slower, I started realizing that my identity had indeed changed. I had given birth to a new me. I had become, as Benjy pointed out at the party, what I never before considered myself: a runner.

You might therefore think that a person who went out running so many times and had no confidence he could finish his three miles, who felt tired at the beginning of these short stints and glad when they were over, would now feel substantially different—at least while running, having garnered the knowledge that he can do 26.2 miles and is now, officially, a "runner." Let me assure you, I don't. The runs are roughly the same. If I always found them tough, particularly at the start, and have always been glad when they're over, I still do and am. And if you think this possibly a function of its being not quite a month since having done it, of my not yet having recovered, I don't think so. I had a remarkable post-race recuperation, with a little muscle and joint soreness immediately. But to everyone's amazement, I wasn't hobbling that night or next day as many would have expected. I could walk up three flights to my son's brownstone apartment without a forklift. I could walk down subway steps on Monday without the assistance of a home attendant. I saw patients that week and could lift myself out of my chair to see them to the door without audible groaning.

I don't understand why. Despite my inclinations but because I was afraid not to, I had trained, and that, perhaps, might explain the quick snap-back. But I certainly didn't know that I'd miss the wall, that I wouldn't cramp as I was supposed to and as both my sons did somewhere in those last four miles a couple of times, that I wouldn't need all those distracting mental devices I was preparing. Maybe it was looking forward to the champagne. Maybe it was the champagne. Who knows? I'm not complaining.

But as soon as I say that nothing, particularly having to do with running, is different, I realize I've also experienced quite the opposite. Two days after my first postmarathon run, I ran on a treadmill and immediately felt much more confident. It actually shocked me. I'm never confident. With anything. Certainly not with running. My pattern when I get on those things has been to reach my pace quickly, but then to worry whether I'll be able to keep it up. I often have had to slow a bit, even after the first half-mile, particularly after not having run in a while. So I was sure the same would be true this time since I hadn't kept that pace, my faster indoor pace, for many weeks. But *au contraire*, it felt fine and I immediately knew I could keep it up. And the difference wasn't that I was consciously telling myself I've done 26, so three should be a snap. I wasn't telling myself anything. I just knew I could do it. I can keep this up. And I will.

Here then is an immediate lesson, not just the ironic one, *plus ça change*, etc., but—take note cynics, curmudgeons, historians—that things actually do change sometimes. I've now come to realize that on certain days things are no different from before, but at the same time, or rather at different times, they are, and that means, as was true before, that no two days or runs are the same.

And that reflection offers the biggest clue as to why this undertaking came to mean so much to me. Despite a lifetime of looking at everyone, particularly myself, through a psychological lens, I have discovered a bit about me through running. And that is not a minor conclusion, since it validates why I've long been interested in sport and, even as I make fun of its practitioners, the psychology of sport.

If I could plunge into this arena (or jump or sidestep or dance into it) and generate as many reflections outside of the arena but because of the arena, I would feel I had accomplished something. We usually think of applying lessons in only one direction. But I want to do it the other way, an attempt I'll also elaborate on in later chapters. From sport we can learn, even teach, some of the basic lessons of psychology, from motivation to learning, from personality to social psychology, from perception to abnormalities. It's grandiose, but it's also mundane.

As a relatively minor example, I remember at mile ten or so near the end of Brooklyn I was thrown off stride by a couple of corner cutters, who were actually shortening the course by running on the sidewalk when we veered through a few consecutive right-angle turns. Now, I've been a corner cutter all my life. When I'm doing errands throughout Manhattan, I've been know to calculate which blocks to walk down and which across. I mark papers and fill out insurance claims on the subway and when I'm in the bathroom for more than a quick visit. I was the only one on line in that pre-Verrazano Bridge corral with a crossword. What else are you going to do with that time? But I didn't cut those sidewalk corners. I thought it cheating. I wanted to play it straight.

Trivial as it may sound, that was a lesson for me: When I cut corners and when I don't. (And if you think I'm mixing the literal with the metaphorical, you're getting the idea. As I'll be arguing throughout, the value of studying running—as sport, as so many other things—is in learning about the metaphor.) In short, the cutting-corners example provides what my philosopher friends call a meta-lesson, a lesson about lessons. They abound in this activity. We can learn about ourselves, even if we don't set records, even if we don't exaggerate the effects of the experience, from something as boring and mundane as running. We cannot only apply the lessons of psychology to sport, but the lessons of sport to everyday life, including its psychology. I am hoping that while these lessons are scattered throughout these pages and some are summarized at the end, you don't have to be running a marathon to find them.

Here's another example. Two days ago I found myself on a treadmill worrying that a lens would pop out of my glasses' frame, because it had done so before, out of the blue, as I sat quietly poring over my notes or oatmeal. I knew it was loose. As I was running, I felt myself out of breath more often than usual and thought it might be due to this anxiety. I kept hoping I'd be able to reach my modest three-mile objective. When finally, at 2.6 miles, the lens did come out and, to my chagrin, rolled down the belt and lodged somewhere underneath the machine, I now, despite my concern and myopia, found myself running better. The worst, it seemed, was over. And while I was still anxious to complete the run and look for the lens, it was a different anxiety. Before, I had an uncertainty. Now I simply had a goal. That, I believe, is an instance of how clarity (even nearsighted clarity) helps. Even with an unpleasant prospect—picking up a probably broken eyeglass lens— knowing what you're doing and where you're going, including being familiar with the terrain, will make it easier.

I don't want to give the impression that every run is in some sense successful or yields a myriad of insights. But I must say, though I think myself essentially finished with running, here it is more than a month after completing the marathon, and during today's run of four miles I almost had an epiphany. I wouldn't go so far as to say I enjoyed it, but for the first time outdoors in quite a while, I didn't feel much stress or pain. And I know the reason. I had decided to combine running with a number of errands, stopping at the bank, the library, and the post office. As a result, I had to stop a few times to take care of quick two- to five-minute business. The only time I've done this before was to attend to bodily urgencies. So did I feel better because of the interruptions? Was it the way one is supposed to warm up that I never do?

I don't think so. I hate doing just one thing. It harkens back to my corner-cutting characteristic. I never go into another room without having at least two objectives. Get the Scotch tape but bring back the running shoes. I don't open the refrigerator without taking at least three things out, inventing needs if I have to. And when they go back, the refrigerator-receivables have company. Imports get combined with exports.

Running, all this time, may have been particularly unpleasant partly because it's really only one thing—spinning one's wheels, as it were. What are you doing when it's over except getting back to the starting point? Okay, okay, Verrazano Bridge to Tavern on the Green was an exception. But if I'm going to run, I'd better be getting somewhere.

Hooray! Not only am I now a runner, I understand myself better through running. I actually accomplished something today with my running and felt better throughout the day, despite the usual: The unreturned phone calls, the junk mail, the belligerent, noncommunicative, and manipulative patients. Running is not just about running, particularly when it includes other activities besides running.

Now it is not surprising that one activity may teach us about others. It is, in fact, as I will attempt to explain in various sections, an intrinsic part of clinical wisdom: the transferential principle. And not just in the therapeutic room. As you behave in one situation, so we presume you will likely behave in another. This, according to a staunch defender of psychoanalysis, as well as a neurological expert (so you know he's no idle theorist), Drew Westen, is a major contribution of Freud's.[6]

But it makes all the more sense for running to be an activity

---

6 D. Westen. *Psychology: Brain, Behavior and Culture (3rd ed.)*. Cambridge, MA: Cambridge University Press; 2002.

which produces these lessons because of what I confirmed during this project and will probably state more than once, that there are as many definitions for "run" as for any word in the language. The Webster's Third New International Dictionary, Unabridged of 2002 has three entire columns, over 100 lines each, of definitions. And that's before we get to the hyphenated ones (a "run-down" in baseball, a "run-in" with the police) or composites (a "runaway" train) or two word phrases ("running expenses," "running mates") or expressions that are related but don't make specific use of the word ("getting off track," or "being on course," or … "cutting corners").

I've devoted a chapter to exploring specifically what that metaphor means, but the concept permeates all the thoughts and pages. Running is not simply about putting one foot rapidly in front of another. My hope was that in the long run, while I feared getting too run down, I didn't want just to run through this, but perhaps in due course, and on this course, I too could formulate a few ideas to run by the reader. And in fact, without consciously intending it, I ran into "run" quite a bit while thinking about this book and writing it.

So if I can keep it up, a running tally, I mean to indicate whenever I run into (come upon) this word its relevant meaning in parentheses, so long as it doesn't mean I'm running (heading off in the direction of) amok. Or something like that. I'm not sure amok is a destination, but if it isn't, it should be. Since it appears I do so much on the run (hastily, without taking time to sit down and digest)—from drinking (I've learned to squeeze the cup and time-manage the gulps), to eating (I haven't yet figured out how to sleep on the run, but I'm sure some of my students can be of assistance), to planning the next party's menu, to balancing the checkbook, to rehearsing lectures or scripts (I once did a stand-up comedy routine and found talking into a small tape recorder as I was rushing somewhere a time-saving device for memorizing)—it occurred to me as I was walking home after playing tennis that if I didn't jot down ideas as soon as they appeared, they'd run off (escape) on their own and hide forever. Particularly for those of us over the age of 50. Or 40. Or 30? In many ways, that ephemeral thought is like the dream you're sure you'll never forget until you wake up in the morning and then can't remember a thing. I advise patients to keep a pad by the bedside and hope they can decipher the scribbles later.

So yes, I now write on the run, sometimes literally slowing to a walk and grabbing the pen and notepaper in my pocket or wrist apparatus. Byron is reputed to have written his best poems on horseback, and since in that position you presumably have to hold a rein or two, this hands-free activity would seem to be much easier. Although on crowded New York streets you might in this manner run into (meet) trouble or your fellow pedestrians. Gestalt Psychologists often cited the environment of the "three Bs"(Bed, Bath, and Bus) as promoting creativity—something about the silence or soothing motion—and so many runners or writers about running cite the run as the fount of their creativity (Jeff Galloway, for instance, repeatedly[7]) that, bizarre as it may seem, the pad or tape recorder in someone's palm as he darts up hills may soon be no weirder than those ubiquitous cell phones that were being sported not just by some two million spectators at the marathon, but by many of the runners themselves.

---

7 J. Galloway. *Training Journal.* Atlanta, GA: Phidippides; 1998.

2

Running's Getting a Good Run— Recent Popularity

Let me say this very simply: You can live life on the run, you can live it quietly and contemplatively; you can live it with great distance, emotionally or cognitively, from what impels your behavior, you can live it with great awareness of what you're doing; and if you listen to all the advice on running (indeed, on sport) that you've gotten or are likely to get, chances are you've heard it all. I referred in the previous chapter to how my own experience running taught me different things, and how these things were sometimes contradictory. As soon as I learned one lesson (e.g., nothing is so different after the marathon from what it was before), I found I couldn't even rely on that because sometimes things were quite different.

So here we have it, from authority. Pay attention, but let it go. We're extremely rational beings, but we get everywhere by letting our unconscious take over, or rather by seeing how many of our important decisions are made unconsciously, immediately, without much concern for the permutations or calculations of the data.[8] Immerse yourself in the activity. Take time off. Surround yourself with others. Do your own thing. Stay away from caffeine. Coffee's good for you.[9]

All of this is worth noting because it highlights the amount of publicity given to running in the media in recent years. The widespread attention is certainly consistent with that being paid to sport in general, interest that is not simply a result either of scandal or of big business. Yes, a *New York Times Magazine* cover-story a decade ago, with the provocative come-on, "Why Sports Don't Matter Anymore," pronounced sport defunct in the aftermath of such travesties as those displayed by Mike Tyson, Tonya Harding, Darryl Strawberry, and the like.[10] The public was subjected to the abuse of professional athletes (was it simply the spitting at fans seeking autographs, or another former "idol" being arrested for gambling or assault?), while in everyday schoolyards and arenas the gruesome and sometimes tragic tales of hockey or soccer dads had become almost commonplace. And while each subsequent year has seen its fair share of drug or steroid abuse from top professionals to high-school adolescents, sport's worldwide popularity is still unmistakable and continues to grow. Billions watched the last Olympic soccer finals. The playoffs between the Yankees and Red Sox was a drama of epic, historical proportions and will be talked about for generations. The Super Bowl each year remains a major event, taken advantage of by advertisers but

---

8   M. Gladwell. *Blink.* New York: Little, Brown & Co.; 2005 (particularly pp. 17, 63, 86).

9   K. McAuliffe. "Enjoy!" *U.S. News and World Report:* Dec. 26, 2005; p. 68. The entire issue was devoted to "50 Ways to Improve Your Life," offering advice while at the same time telling us not to pay attention to studies since "most findings are false," a result of bias or poor design.

10 R. Lipsyte. "The Emasculation of Sports." *New York Times Magazine:* April 2, 1995; pp. 50–57.

having a scope going beyond beer drinkers and Janet Jackson voyeurs. And there were over 37,000 runners in the last two New York Marathons, making it the biggest run anywhere.

So it's not surprising that we're subject to a lot of information. Or that much of it is as contradictory as "Basic *Monday Night Football* Lessons for Wives" gaining in attendance just as *Monday Night Football* was about to fade away from the broadcast lineup. In fact, the past year alone saw an abundance of articles written on aspects of running, even repetitions in the same paper. Granted, when the New York Marathon is imminent, it's understandable; but practically every week for the last six months there has been some major article on hyponatremia, or on aged runners, or on former criminals or addicts who had become runners, or handicapped runners … and how I longed for the important comment on what the frequency of all this indicated, that running is not simply about running anymore, or perhaps never was.

Yes, two articles in the *New York Times* itself on how too much water is dangerous for you.[11,12] And another on how too much exercise is not good.[13] And another on how overtraining is common and leads to injuries in the young.[14] I can tell you from personal experience that when I decided to rest for a day after running fourteen in a row, I did not miss it nor think about it once all day. No doubt you can be excessive, but I can't believe all those 2000-mile-a-week guys, those seven-marathons-in-seven-days-on-seven-continent guys, are all madmen (well, maybe the first group) who don't know their own bodies.

11 G. Kolata. "Study Cautions Runners to Limit Their Water Intake." *New York Times:* April 14, 2005; p. A1

12 G. Kolata. "Marathoners Warned About Too Much Water." *New York Times:* Oct. 20, 2005; p. D7.

13 J. Brody. "Fit Is One Thing; Obsessive Exercise Is Another." *New York Times:* Aug. 9, 2005; p. F7

14 B Pennington. "Doctors See a Big Rise in Injuries as Young Athletes Train Nonstop." *New York Times:* Feb. 22, 2005; p. D7.

Fanatics about this stuff, maybe. A religious experience, perhaps. But that doesn't make the fundamentalists of the racecourse the suicide bombers of their own bodies. And that same *Times* will herald the 70 year-old who goes to a match race in Holland, no less, with a contemporary who does 100 a week and sub-three hour marathons.

We are, according to the latest, made for running; indeed, for long-distance running. Only horses, hyenas, and dogs are capable of anything like the marathons humans run.[15] We're not as fast as the ostrich or cheetah, but they can't match our endurance. Attention given to the evolutionary history of running has indicated some of the reasons. There are probably two dozen features of the body that help us, from our legs to trunk to arms. And yet, you can also do such significant damage. Why is everyone so concerned with the knees? Because runners have destroyed them. And not because they weren't doing it right or training enough or stretching right. Some of the most accomplished and dutiful have had the problem too. The body gave out somewhere, despite the careful grooming.

Considering that the body has received all this attention, why did the next question not get asked? Probably too politically incorrect. Are women runners different from men? Dare we say it? Is it all a matter of upbringing and role play? Of course, to a degree. Kathryn Switzer, one of the major spokeswomen for the sport, who is credited with breaking down the gender barrier in Boston, told me she was grateful to her family, one that included lots of brothers, for failing to distinguish her potential from theirs. Her father, in fact, brought sport into all their lives, so she never contemplated her future as a cheerleader. But women in my study also, as they get older, do not generally consider themselves athletes as much as men. They've either got more to do somehow, despite all our gen-

---

15 J. Wilford. "Running Extra Mile Sets the Human Apart." *New York Times:* November 18, 2004; p. A24.

der-equality progress, or else the finding implies something else—a kind of aggression, even if it's not directed at others, of which perhaps women do have less.

Not too many years ago, Maccoby and Jacklyn summarized gender differences in a major book.[16] While differences in children such as verbal ability (girls better) and mathematical ability (boys better) do persist somewhat into adulthood and may be based on brain or hormonal differences, there is also—perhaps obviously—a gap in aggression. Inject testosterone into male rats and they attack each other more. But women, some may have noted, can be violent too. I have a colleague who's collected all the instances and studies of women abusing men, even physically, and he claims there are more of these than the other way around—especially more unreported ones, since men are loath to lodge the complaint. (For my next book, I will detail the results of 2000 years of research, only some of it on the couch, on the gender question, including everything from the meaning of smiling on entering elevators to saying good evening when leaving elevators. But for the moment, I'll restrict the observations to a section of the racecourse.)

I have noticed on a couple of occasions when I was volunteering during races that there's a decided difference in how men and women approach the water tables. If a man doesn't get what he wants immediately, he's apt to become petulant or outright hostile, cursing the lack of service or immediate service or proper service ("No Gatorade!?!"). And I must say I'm no exception. There were a couple of times during my marathon when the tables weren't quite ready or the cups not filled, and rather than interrupt my pace for another second, I became quite agitated and verbal. (I was always under the impression that if I stopped running, no matter for how

---

16 E. Maccoby and C. Jacklin. *The Psychology of Sex Differences.* Stanford, CA: Stanford U. Press; 1974.

briefly, I wouldn't be able to start again, so when I came up behind some slower runners on a narrow approach to the Bronx bridge, for example, I did a fair amount of dodging and muttering—even a bark or two—to clear my path.) In fact, there were so many do-gooders at the end of Brooklyn just before the halfway mark, handing out everything from Kool-Aid to paper towels, that even when a cute preadolescent fumbled a bit with her Scott extra strength roll, I grumbled. Women, on the other hand, (the "More" marathon, begun in 2004 for women over 40 and allowing pairs of women to do a half each, was a prime example of this) showed great pleasure and appreciation at the oases, not only thanking us but also taking the time to say "Thank you for volunteering." And they smile more.

Is this cooperativeness unique to running? Perhaps. At the uppermost levels of professional tennis, women apparently don't want to practice with one another. The top men will hit with one another, but for the women there appears to be more of a competitive dilemma. And it isn't only a matter of seeking out male hitters for greater competition. They're reluctant to show each other what they've got.

But aggression is not only a matter of clobbering or yelling at someone. It's also a matter of clearing a path, literally and figuratively. Yes, women ask for directions more, even when they don't have to. The sign at the foot of the escalator clearly says "shoes, 2nd floor," but they will ask the guard, "Where are the shoes?" And they will interrupt more. And change more. No matter what the relative number of people in my therapeutic calendar at the moment, women will effect 95 percent of the changes in appointments. And they're more frequently no-shows, particularly the new patients. The first appointment is always a bit iffy, especially as more and more patients come from HMOs where they're apparently encouraged to reach three or more doctors to see who's most compatible. (They now give workshops in the therapeutic sales-manship game, including give-away promotions and reduced prices for "members." Pretty soon I expect to hear recommendations of what to have on the stove to be most conducive to the therapeutic alliance, much as real-estate brokers advise simulating baking cookies by putting a little cinnamon and sugar in a warming pan before prospective buyers appear.) But women seem to be about twice as likely not to show as men. And of course not showing is also a form of aggression, like not calling or not doing what one says she'll do. But it's passive aggression, the resource of those unwilling or afraid to be direct. Which is why it was so nice when my would-be tennis partner—who got me into playing years ago—didn't just say "Let's play sometime," but offered "How about Sunday at nine?" And actually showed up ... again and again.

3

Run It Up the Sport Flagpole and See Who Salutes It— Sport "Analysis"

When a friend told me she'd just read a book on "fasting," I stared at her in disbelief. There are books on fasting? What is there to say beyond two simple words?

And when I first started running and thinking about running and thinking about writing about running, I felt similarly. (And judging from the look on peoples' faces when I tell them what I'm doing, many feel quite the same.) Perhaps there are some fitness fanatics, maybe even with a psychological bent, who, having discovered a healthy form of exercise, believe that there's probably a few more things to say about running than "Don't Eat!" But a sport? Football's a sport. Lacrosse may even be a sport. Tennis—now there's a sport about which there are a few things to say. So much so that I even wrote a book about it, and my bookstore and library indicate there have been a few others.

But running?[17]

With tennis, if you'll allow me this diversion, I was intrigued by what I thought to be its psychological dimensions and started finding them everywhere. I discovered and implemented strategies about when to hit where, when to take risks, how to play the score, how to recognize and control or not control emotions, and how to deal with manipulative or talkative or passive-aggressive opponents or—heaven help us!—gracious and solicitous ones. I was also convinced that other notably "macho" sports—football, basketball, hockey—were less about testosterone than about decision making, about thinking and thinking about what the other guy or team is thinking, dynamics that illustrate how psychological the most physical competition can be.

You have to be aware, of course, of the salient dimensions and attend to them, because otherwise you'll lapse into what I call the "Sport Pundit Phenomenon," illustrated best by former-quarterback-cum-TV-analysts but including everyone

---

17 With the recent advent of "cardio tennis," it seems important to distinguish exercise from sport, although I must say that it's a distinction more honored in the breach than in the observance. Most graduate sport-psychology programs, indeed the division of the APA itself, call themselves the Sport and Exercise Psychology Branch. If running around a tennis court trying to hit the ball didn't seem enough exercise to these fitness people, it now seems you must include a real "cardio" workout as well. As you can doubtless tell, I'm not convinced. Maybe we should incorporate something with tennis balls (juggling?) as we jog around our paths. I don't think we need be so concerned with putting the exercise back in sport. (Except perhaps for golf. Ahh, but there's all that walking. Right. And that's the point as well. If golf is a sport, it's like walking plus darts. I'd rather walk to the pub and find a dartboard.) If anything, let's concentrate on putting the sport back into exercise. The point is that there's a lot more to sport than simply exercise, as there's a lot more to thought than naming all of Shakespeare's plays. A decent warm-up for the gray matter perhaps, enough to get one started, but little more.

from journalists to coaches to even current quarterbacks between plays, it seems. Here's Peyton Manning "explaining" why his Indianapolis Colts suddenly lost after winning thirteen games in a row and looking as if they could go undefeated in the '05 season: "They [the San Diego Chargers] have good players." He then adds, "We didn't do what we normally do." (Variation A: "… are capable of doing;" Variation B; "execute.") You might as well say, "because the other team scored more points." Here's Troy Brown, after his fumble, explaining why the New England Patriots' streak of ten playoff wins in a row came to an end at the hands of the Denver Broncos: "You have to take care of the ball." Here's Tom Brady, the quarterback who'd never lost one of those games: "We didn't play our best." And, on greater reflection: "We didn't take it to them." A bit later on we might hear some more "in-depth" analysis, mesmerizing us with talk about the "line" dominating the other "line" ("submission" apparently doesn't win in this sport), or one player's having an "outstanding" game. And here's Venus Williams explaining her first-round loss in the 2006 Olympics to an unknown Bulgarian teenager: "I didn't bring it with me." (Your racquet? Your hair beads? Your mojo?) "I couldn't get it right." It's similar to explaining the outcome of a tennis match by referring to "breaks of serve." Yes, you can win without such "domination," but it's rare. The question is, why did the breaks occur, or why did the team suddenly have five turnovers when they did? Did Andy Roddick just relieve the tension in a "marathon" match against Younes El Anyaoui by sitting down on the court? Did Nadal just run down a ball he wasn't supposed to? Did Novotna just realize she might win and start shaking? A little more depth, pundits, a little more realization that the Aristotelian distal causes challenge our intellects a bit more than the proximate. Did I fall because I wasn't looking? Or because I was looking, but at someone else?

Or because someone else had just prompted my looking somewhere else? I've always been impressed with the "fake," a maneuver in sport that most everywhere else in life, at least in our public-relations releases, is considered cheating or even "dirty." We don't, as a rule, admire people who are fakes, although they may capture our imagination in literature precisely because they are not real (all the mistaken identities or disguises or imposters in Shakespeare, the twins or lookalikes exchanging places in *The Prince and the Pauper* and *A Tale of Two Cities,* the great imposter *Tartuffe,* The "Ernests" in Oscar Wilde, Cyrano pretending to Roxanne his words are Christian's, or Christian pretending he spoke them). Their appeal probably lies in their enacting for us some unconscious desire to be someone else, or to be outrageous and get away with everything. The word "personality" itself (from the Latin *persona,* meaning, "mask") suggests that our outside is only a cover, a disguise for what's hidden inside. But fake pearls or feigned emotions or fake advertising are not generally what we openly admire. (Okay, we'll accept fake fur, for the animal lovers.) They're false, they're misleading, they're not fair, they're designed to get something out of us we don't want to give, they're promises that won't be kept, they promote our mistrust.

And in so much of sport, they're an essential part of the game. If you know what we're going to do, where we're going to throw the pitch or loft the pass or shoot the puck, you gain the advantage. So in basketball we pretend to shoot to "fake him out of his shoes" and go around him. In tennis, after a long baseline rally, we throw in a drop shot. In football linesmen and receivers are continually bluffing one way and moving another. In the Super Bowl of 2004 a compelling new fake factor was introduced (or at least spoken of to some extent): Tom Brady's eyes. While other quarterbacks fake the handoff and throw the "bomb," Brady does what apparently few others can do—he looks a different way than where he intends to throw. At least, until the last second. Like a pitcher's suddenly throwing to first. Like the old basketball player's "no look" pass. Like a window-shopping or cell-phone-talking pedestrian about to bump into you. Sort of. You think they know where they're walking, but they don't have to. You do. It may be what lawyers and real estate brokers and theatrical agents love: it's poker, the bluff, a playing field where it's fair to be a fake—in fact, it's necessary to succeed. Who knows what the other side is up to? Who knows what they're trying to get away with? Who knows what the real price is? You don't want your competitors to outguess you. You thought I was going there, as Billy Crystal says in *Mr. Saturday Night,* but I went there. It's the essence of humor. You thought I was about to shoot, so I passed.

And as these sports develop their intricate maneuvers, the rules are not unlike those fine distinctions that Talmudic scholars or Supreme Court justices are in the business of making. Was the play over or was it a fumble? Sixteen replays before deciding whether he had possession before he went down, or whether his feet were in bounds before he was pushed out or whether—take heed now, referees—he was making a "football move" when he coughed up the ball. Was Giant running back Tiki Barber down before he ran another 30 yards for the crucial touchdown against the Kansas City Chiefs? It depends on whether his knee was touching the ground. That depends on where the ground was. That blade of grass (or turf nap?) sticking up between the defender's shoes on which his knee may have been otherwise resting? Was it a balk? It depends on whether his left foot was above his left wrist when he twirled and threw to first. Was it interference? It depends on whether he left his declared path before he collided. Was it a blocking foul or a charge? It depends on whether or not the defense had "established position" (rather than just being "immobile," as in days of yore—two years ago; modifications abound as the collisions mount). Was it three points or two? Fifteen minutes and sixteen blowups of the last shot when Kentucky tied Michigan State to get to the 2005 NCAA Final Four were necessary to determine whether the foot was over the line or not. And what, in fact, did they show? It was tangent! Is a tangent touching the circle? You bet. But, by definition, at only one point. So is touching at one point on it? Over it? Does a point even exist? Hey, I remember geometry. A point is nondimensional. It exists only in Platonic heaven.

In spite of these being questions that may be answerable, or perhaps because of this, they also make so much of sport intriguing. These are matters, as I've just tried to illustrate, into the ambiguities of which one can dig like a gold prospector searching for the mother lode. Should he have gone shallow or deep? These are sports that can be as aesthetic as they are physical (Michael Strahan of the Giants talks of his "game within a game" with linesman Jon Runyon of the Eagles as a "dance"), as one watches the point guard or receiver soar in balletic fashion, or twist left, then right. And these are sports where psychology can surely play a role. He thinks I'll hit the ball elsewhere since I served it to his forehand last time and he clobbered it, so I won't—I'll hit it the same way. Outplaying the opposition so often means "outsmarting" one's opponent or staying one psychological or strategic step ahead. The hockey rink as chessboard.

But, as I began to say five pages ago, running? Twenty-five books on the shelves of Barnes and Noble, last I looked. That's before we get to the sport psychologists and/or the academics writing a few words about it. What are they saying? Even before the running "boom" a generation ago, even as we look at the great number of articles written about it recently, this sport, this activity, this masochistic exercise has had a history, as evidenced by some "classic" works. And where does psychology fit?

The Complete Book of Running has two pages on psychology, essentially about "positive thinking" (i.e., believe you can) and promoting relaxation to concentrate, an apparently good thing.[18] Except that then there are a few words about "dissociating," which would seem to be the opposite of concentrating (unless you're supposed to concentrate on something other than running, but that does sound a lot like being distracted, which sounds a lot like the opposite of concentrating). And time and again one hears about what to me has now become the all-too-familiar emphasis on two psychological messages—"visualization" and "breaking the race down into parts." I say "familiar" because in sport psychology visualization has become the one thing on which investigators seem to be able to get a handle, and of which they can more or less demonstrate the efficacy. When just before what was to become my "marathon" achievement, I was to give a talk to the New York Road Runners on "psychological issues," it had to be renamed "Visualization," for fear that the running audience couldn't, as the medical director told me, deal with anything deep or "historical;" they just wanted practical advice that could help them in the race. My experience since then is quite different. People want to know what's true, and we sell our clients, patients, and athletes short when we limit ourselves to behavioral Band-Aids. I even had a great deal of difficulty with certain members of my "psyching team" when I advocated principles other than pasting a piece of finishing-line ribbon (phony ribbon, I might add, since the finish line hasn't had a ribbon for years) on runners' shirts as a talisman which they could actually rub like the genie's lamp for magical help when the going got tough during the race. It wasn't that I objected if people had an itch for this sort of thing. Indeed, the president of the Sport Psychology Division of the

18 A. Burfoot. *Runner's World Complete Book of Beginning Running.* Emmaus, PA: Rodeale; 2005 (particularly pp. 200–202).

American Psychological Association wrote a front-page article three years ago in the newsletter heralding the value of just such a ribbon as a means of encouragement.[19] I just couldn't believe that with psychology having been around for 100 or 2000 years, depending on when you start counting, that was the best we had to offer. And that second point about breaking things down was indeed a mental device of long-standing importance, one that I myself was later to find very helpful. But was that it?

On the MSN website cover page some weeks ago, sport psychologist John Murray emphasized the importance of resiliency (recovering from the loss of a point), reducing distraction (it could be personal, the crowd, even the media), and the pattern of taking little steps. I note this because of the mixture. Suddenly, without much connection but as if there were a connection, there's also advice on relaxing and the old standby, imagery. This from the expert who's later cited in *Tennis–TV Magazine* for putting an hour's worth of his coaching on eBay and getting a $250 offer (not so extraordinary considering what some other gurus, alcoholic counselors without credentials, are commanding in some circles these days).[20] He is also the coach of Vince Spadea, and is reportedly responsible for helping him to end the longest losing streak in the history of professional tennis. A similar report explains Conchita Martinez's resurgence in the 2000 French Open as being due to her working with a sport psychologist. What did he do for her? She "explains" it in her postmatch interview: He taught her how to relax, practice breathing, and feel good about herself. The question is not only how much of this stuff is there and how much of it is true, but how much is psychology and how much can be applied to running?

19 K. Hays. "Giving Sport Psychology Away." *ESPNews (Exercise and Sport Psychology Newsletter* APA, Division 47): 16 (2); Fall 2002.

20 *Tennis Week–TV:* Jan.–Feb., 2006; p. 91.

Then there is the opposite side of this pseudoscientific spectrum, those authors who sound like Human Potential Movement graduates as they attest to using "spiritual resources" (lots of praying?) or refer to the Runner's Inner Cosmic Being, the "mystical ... the dance ... embracing and flowing in fatigue ... transcending limits ... the journey ... the positive ... the warrior within, detaching." [21,22]

Be a deer, be a bird.

Thanks. Now that I'm getting used to kale and figs sprinkled with flaxseeds on the dinner plate, I'm looking forward to grass and worms for dessert.

When I first began to contemplate running, I resembled the worst of my patients, doubting that this activity had any merit at all (or would-be patients, since the most skeptical don't usually show up in the office for more than a minute, when their wives or significant others or the courts order them or drag them in). Furthermore, why was it that with all those books on the shelves, and the relatively small mention of psychology, everyone was now agreeing how important the mental is? What does it mean when a prospective marathoner, interviewed by a newscaster during the last New York heat wave about how she feels running in 98-degree weather, says, "Well this is all mental anyway"? And those seven pounds I lost in my last August training run? Could I have wished them away through meditation? Is that what we'd mean by calling dieting "mental?" Mentally melting away the mental grams of mental fat? Oh sure, some lip service is always given to the head or heart being the most important thing, much more in charge than the legs or lungs, but scarcely a mention of what that means. Plenty of references to letting the mental energy take over, or that the second half of the marathon is where it all

---

21 J. Galloway. *Marathon.* Atlanta, GA: Phidippedes; 2000 (p. iii).

22 J. Lynch and W. Scott. *Running Within.* Champaign, IL: Human Kinetics; 1999 (p. 95).

begins, or that the last six miles are totally about the mind. (Remember Boris Becker on "marathon" tennis matches? "The fifth set is not about tennis.") Yeah, yeah. It's about "who wants it more." And how do you know who wants it more? You see who wins. As if James Blake, in last year's match for the ages with Andre Agassi, didn't want it because he lost by the smallest of margins, a two-point differential in the tie breaker of the fifth set.

Even Bob Glover, author of many a running bible, leader of many training classes at the Road Runners, and my most reliable source for simple marathon schedule information, falls into this second kind of trap;[23] what I, a psychologist, would call the "Psychological Seduction Trap." On the one hand we have the Neanderthals who believe that all psychology is, at best, unprovable myths to justify psychologists' existence. And on the other, we have individuals given to statements like "if you think it's so, it is so." Even nutrition studies are proving contradictory, so is that mental too? If you think it works, it will work? More chocolate cake, please—I believe calories don't count! I've convinced myself that vodka helps. I now drink a liter of it before a race!

And once again we meet those sport psychologists. At the 1980 Olympics, there was reportedly one. In the 2004 games in Athens, there were over 100. Within the popular arena we're hearing that, for example, Robby Ginepri, the up-and-coming U.S. tennis player who made it to the semifinals of the U.S. open last year, reportedly had hired one, and suddenly, after having been knocked out of the previous three "slam" tournaments in the first round, turned his career around and beat three seeded players (Haas, Gasquet, and Coria) in a few days. What did the coach tell him? Be mentally tough. Focus. Stay Positive. (When Ginepri lost in the first round of the 2006 Australian Open, as he had been

23 B. Glover. *The Runner's Handbook.* New York: Penguin; 1996.

doing in slam tournaments all the previous year, commentator Brad Gilbert explained that "He just lost it," after blowing his two-set-to-love lead. No mention was made of the location of his sport psychologist.)

And yet, these pearls may reflect more wisdom than what's cast by the academicians. Running's there—occupying about one percent of their investigations or theories—but the basic problem, as I see it, is that no one has clarified the relationship of these two separate entities contained in the vessel of sport psychology.

The most obvious approach is applying psychology to sports. That would seem to be the assumption behind the older fields of applied psychology. Industrial, educational, forensic, consumer, even clinical psychology each purport to take a principle uncovered in psychology's laboratory and apply it to the factory or classroom or courtroom or supermarket. People are apt to be harsher on their own kind? The defense, contrary to expectation, should prefer women as jurors in the Kobe Bryant rape case. Peoples' moods are affected by the colors of the rainbow? Package your breakfast cereals in yellow.

But is it not equally feasible, and perhaps more interesting, to go the other way; to show, in effect, that the discoveries in the sports arena can be applied elsewhere, even to the entire spectrum of psychology's domain, to our thinking, feeling and interacting in the four corners of life? Does not the cover of that introductory psychology book, displaying a picture of runners crossing the finish line, imply that all psychology can be considered sport?[24] (My colleague actually wants to teach introductory psychology as sport psychology, since all the relevant themes of the former can be found in the latter.) Perhaps we want to say that all sport is psychology? I doubt

---

23 M. Gazzaniga and T. Heatherton. *Psychological Science: Mind, Brain, and Behavior.* New York: W. W. Norton; 2003.

that, but some—see below—fall into that temptation. Maybe they're simply parallel. These possibilities are reminiscent of what used to be referred to in philosophical circles as the "mind-body" problem. Monists would argue that while these two substances appear very different, one is reducible to the other. Either everything is matter (materialism) or everything is a mental representation (idealism). Either it's all in the velocity and configuration of the neurons, or it's all in the heart and head. Dualists believe that one causes the other (interactionists), to wit, anxiety causes poor performance or "chemical imbalance" causes depression.

And speaking of depression, this is often my reaction when I listen to conference presentations by researchers into the field, since it appears that in putting academic psychology into sport, we've taken the sport out of sport. There's lots of attention paid to academic constructs like mindfulness or hardiness or meta-cognitive strategies, a veritable hodgepodge of esoteric findings. And there's little to put it together. We know an awful lot, as philosophical psychologist Daniel Robinson once said, about what doesn't matter. This division also holds true for psychology as a whole. On the one hand you have the physiologists who want to make psychology biology. And on the other there are the spiritualists who want to make it all philosophy. And those are, in fact, its two parents. But the child is no longer a neonate or even an adolescent, and needs to find its own identity.

One corroboration for the importance of sport can be found in the emphasis placed on overall health, one that was paramount at the most recent psychology convention I had attended. But no one in one seminar seems to know enough about the others, even when there's a theme that might unite them. Men and depression? Yes, have them exercise. The "whole person" health routine? There should obviously be no "mind-body dichotomy," à la Descartes. "Positive psychology?"

A natural. If you make people optimistic, they'll forgo their bad addictions. It's even startling how directly athletics comes up on panels having nothing to do with sport. "Take athletes," says the speaker on "Flourishing." It's like reaching a "high." The most integrated presentation was actually given by Trisha Meili *(I Am the Central Park Jogger)*, who, in her inspirational talk about an incredible journey back to health, demonstrates by her example more psychology than is contained in all the two-by-two designs and supported by statistical analyses of variance.

In short, with all our emphasis on health and its being determined by a combination of the physical and the psychological, there is something too fat and inefficient about academic research, even brilliance, being directed at the mind-body playing field. It's an approach that seems too strained. But there is also something too shallow or lean about stars, coaches, and even journalists taking up the cudgel, since their muscles are so undeveloped. My simple conclusion is that if mind and body invariably work together, if even pathology can be considered an extension of one at the expense of the other, then sport or "play" must be integrated with work, that is, thought. Because, as I'm trying to illustrate, there really is so much to think about.

So with all that as background, I had to then start paying attention, ontologists and metaphysicians notwithstanding, to what was real. To my own running first, like any good psychologist, and to those (particularly, my kids) around me. Take the world as we find it, said the Gestalt psychologists, naively and uncritically, before you go around setting up your elaborate clinics or laboratories. Which is what I tell my Introductory Psychology students. Look around you—that's where a psychologist starts. You don't need to explore the heavens like the astronomer, or wait for the earthquakes like the geologist. Look how people dress or, less obviously, use space and time. Uncover what Edward Hall referred to as *The Hidden Dimension* or *The Silent Language.*[25,26]

So I began with me. The first assumption was that knowing some psychology, if it's worth anything, ought to make you do things better or at least see some things more clearly. (Of course, the cobbler's children are barefoot and all psychologists—as well as their children—are crazy. But still, let's pretend that students of the subject can fare somewhat better than the teachers.) The primary purpose would be to uncover what running can do for us psychologically, but this doesn't simply mean how it helps us feel better or even think more clearly. It means, as stated above, applying its dimensions to other areas. We drink Tang even though we're not astronauts and Gatorade even though we're not Florida "Gators" (for whom, if some didn't know it, they were originally developed). We take a clever immobilizing device designed for use on quarterback Chad Pennington's broken thumb on the playing field, and use a variety of its technology to reduce the chance of pregnant women miscarrying. After all, it's not just the quarterback who carries the ball. Or a pregnant woman who miscarries. And to increase the likelihood of application, if we viewed running—or all of sport, for that matter—as a metaphor, we'd have a handle (or a leg up) on how that application could work.

But here a vital distinction is necessary. I've seen a television commercial recently in which businessmen decide they need an "all-out blitz" to market their product, and a huge linebacker walks by decrying their use of "sport clichés." Yes, they abound. Yes, they're part of what I was referring to earlier as the shallow "interpretation" that purports to explain results but explains nothing. But while a metaphor ("I think this debate may become a marathon") may become a cliché ("I

25 E. Hall. *The Hidden Dimension*. Garden City, NY: Doubleday; 1966.
26 E. Hall. *The Silent Language*. Greenwich, CT: Fawcett; 1959.

don't want to be a Monday-morning quarterback"), the very use of the metaphor shows us the power of the image, one we don't wish summarily to discard lest we throw out the baby with the bathwater (which is both). More about this later.

If this book, therefore, is about running, it's also about not running, and it's through running that I come to see this. Because if it works or is true in running, and we understand why, it should be true in not running. It's about Tang and the quarterback's cast and not miscarrying.

As an example, once again, I start with me. One of the first observations I made—and this startled me because it was such a cliché—was that all days were not the same. I had good runs and bad runs. Yes, surely one hears often enough about the quarterback or tennis player's having an "off" day, but I had always viewed that in sport as a lame excuse for our ignorance. When you don't know what makes the difference, bring in astrology. It's hardly different when one explains a winner as "on a roll" or "in a groove" or in the "zone." All of these seemed just pseudo-explanations, if not for the mysterious causes, then for the obvious—that momentum, whatever that is, grew as a result of being ahead or behind early. It could have been otherwise.

So why, when I heard that Shelly Glover has said at some New York Road Runner workshops that you can expect during the average running week one good day for every four bad, did I eagerly concur? I had felt it. Not that ratio, necessarily. But during the last two days, for example, I had to slow from my usual pace to do three miles, and today I did five relatively easily. With even a little more speed than usual. It's not that I felt it necessary to be great or even good each day. One would do very well. After all, if you're solving Fermat's last theorem or writing an ad for Alka Seltzer or winning Wimbledon or, indeed, running a 3:50 mile, how many do you need? Greatness is not always measured by average or even consistent performance. Once, Roger Banister beat four minutes and became a hero (yes, he did it later too, but it didn't matter).

But still, one wants to know what makes the difference. What was it? The yogurt? The different shoes? The better sleep? Actually, I slept less last night. Why was I so much worse the other day? My shirt was too big; actually it was a sweater I'm not used to. The socks were lumpy. The blister? Or was it because I was on a treadmill and the shorts felt like they were slipping and I was self-conscious because people were next to me? Or did I eat less breakfast, or not drink enough water, or need to urinate? Or was it that today all of life was better, I could run and write and talk and teach and do therapy better, because I was brimming with confidence? And that's why we have psychologists in dugouts and locker rooms. How are things at home, McGuire? Make them better and you'll do better on the field. And if they're not, pretend they are, act "as if."

Should I do scientifically controlled experiments to explain it? Harry Higdon describes his participation in some efforts at experimental studies of the runner.[27] The purpose was to test the effects of fluids and monitor the efficiency of oxygen use. The experimenters were able to reach some conclusions; for example, that drinking on the run seems to help. But then, according to another study, there was no greater benefit for sports drinks over water. But these involved fast runners over a period of less than two hours, and further investigations point out the importance of that time variable since it's not until later that the electrolyte replacement of the sports drinks works better. But the fact that time is a critical variable also affects the other kinds of studies. But, but, but.

Have we gone far enough? Yes, we can show that over twenty years oxygen-intake efficiency decreases, but so does the amount of running and, as Higdon indicates, a basic problem

---

27 H. Higdon. *Masters Running: A Guide to Training and Staying Fit After 40.* Emmaus, PA: Rodale; 2005.

with what's called a correlation study is discovering which has caused which. Is your efficiency less because you're running less, or are you running less because you're efficiency's less? To decide the question, you would need to take two similar groups, control the amount of running they do over twenty years, and then look at the result. (A good example of what limits experimental psychology: We can't do the behavioral study that counts. People aren't rats. Even when they run. Even in a rat race.) Sleep, shoes, yogurt, or a dozen other things—who knows what made it a good run today?

We're thus back to the simpleminded notion of having good or bad days, and before sorting out the infinite potential causes, let's look at it the other way and see if it's not applicable to so many disparate things. Today (a rare day, I'll take one of five) I write fluently, if not effortlessly, the words and ideas flowing. Other days, it's literally like pulling teeth. No words come. They're packed in my gums. It's a mystery. Where are they hiding? And if I drill at them forcibly, they may spill out, or else crack or prove so remote as to be unreachable, at least with my current box of tools.

Perhaps it's relevant here to bring in the well-known self-fulfilling prophecy, a phenomenon having plenty of application throughout psychology. It may even provide the aforementioned "positive psychology" with some empirical or evidentiary backbone. When we expect people to do well in something, like classes, they do. We inspire them to better performance. We reward them when they do well, thus providing motivation, and we ignore them (treating it as ego-alien, perhaps, or simply not really there) when they don't. Ignoring is much better than punishment, since punishment only calls attention to the offence and to many, especially those used to being ignored, it serves as a positive reinforcement. If I can't get my name in the paper (or kindergarten star list) by becoming President (or being good), I'll try to shoot one (or be bad). We thereby verify the important learning principle of focusing on and rewarding good performance while not focusing on bad.

The well-known work *Pygmalion in the Classroom* actually showed that students, equal in potential to others but whom the teacher believed would do well, in fact did.[28] And the others did poorly. It may explain why people who trust therapy get better. They believe they will. It certainly explains why when you call a person smart or pretty or crazy often enough, they become so. Or the opposite. They take pains to stay that way because they believe they can, at least in the case of the positive characteristics.

With their opposites, the opposite is true. Take no pains to be attractive and you won't be. No, you can't make a silk purse out of a sow's ear; but eat poorly, dress poorly, and don't exercise, and you won't exactly be a treat for someone to look upon.

It's even been shown to be true of rats in experiments, lending some doubt to whether our subjects comply with hypotheses, when they can adduce them, rather than prove them in objective fashion. Through some process, coddling of their undersides, perhaps, or treating them roughly, one encourages them to be what one expects.

So is it true of running and sport in general? Of course—it's the motive behind a dutiful, caring parent encouraging a child, or a coach bolstering the belief system of an athlete—but then why aren't we all so wonderful? Lack of support? Even when we get support, we fail. It can't be that simple. If so, those words wouldn't ever be packed in my gums. I'd have positively thought them out.

And it certainly didn't apply to my running. I started with no confidence—for good reason, I'd never done it, couldn't

---

28 R. Rosenthal and L. Jacobson, *Pygmalion in the Classroom*. New York: Holt, Rinehart & Winston; 1981.

do it, only ran to catch a bus or the light before it changed and was always huffing and puffing after half a block. I continued with no confidence. Having achieved some intermediate goals (¼ mile was a first intermediate goal, I kid you not), I never went into a run believing that I'd finish, certainly not without a hitch. And finally, on the eve of what was to be my greatest running achievement, completing a New York Marathon, I would have been happy finishing the same day I started. I'd done the training, I'd heard all the techniques, or at least enough to get me through, particularly the unknown 20–26 mile stretch, and I was sure that, at best, I'd be walking those last six; and at worst, walking the last thirteen; and at worst worst, walking the last 20 after cramping at six; and at worst worst worst, not crossing the bridge without pains and having to be carted off on a sweep bus, forever hiding my head, while envisioning a little blurb in the paper the next day, saying "Sport Psychologist Had Best Stay in the Laboratory."

4

How Do I Run?
Let Me Count the Ways—
The Metaphor

As I often find myself telling patients in their first session, nothing in life falls outside the province of therapy. What I don't tell them, but the astute ones soon discover, is that since I like to play with the metaphor on the couch, even define therapy as the study of the metaphor, I can get carried away. You keep your fists tight? You're expecting a fight. You keep talking about your narrow kitchen? You need to broaden your life. You are so soft spoken as to be inaudible much of the time? Sorry, you want everyone to tune in to your program and turn up the volume. But, and I say this with full self-consciousness, once you start down that metaphoric road there's no turning back. Once you bake your metaphoric cake, you have to eat it. Once you plant your metaphoric garden … you get the idea. We can be so engulfed in metaphors that we can drown in meta-metaphors, metaphors about metaphors, mixed metaphors notwithstanding.

If I can indulge my pedantic predilection for a moment, the metaphor in life, as in literature, is based on a comparison, on a substitution of one thing for another. For something to be a good substitute, however, it obviously must be similar. "Sweet-n'-Low" is not a salt surrogate. Stepparents have problems because the kids won't see or allow the similarity to the parent being displaced. (They're either a poor substitute or too good a substitute.) The "sixth man" on the basketball team is most useful when he can blend imperceptibly into or extend the driving force for which he's substituting.

So the power of the metaphor is determined by how forcibly the similarity breaks through the difference and how, once the poet reconciles the two parties, there can be no more separation (to mix a few more). Yes, we know time flies; but how much more poignant that "its winged chariot is drawing near" (Andrew Marvell), or that "the bird of time has but a little way to flutter" (*The Rubaiyat of Omar Khayyam*)? Yes, we know that people will go to extremes to make their point, but that "the devil can cite scripture for his purpose" (Shakespeare) hammers it home. In fact, we "hammer" that point across because we're not just making it, we're not just tapping it, we're applying some force to try and get it to stay, like a nail into wood. When we come into money and a "weight is lifted from our shoulders," it is indeed as if some physical burden has been removed so that we needn't so strenuously have to bear (shoulder) our responsibility.

There is in fact probably no part of the body which is not used as a substitute for some other, more abstract activity, whether it's giving someone a hand, keeping one's chin up, or toeing the line. And not just the visible, tangible parts of the body are called into front-line metaphoric action. We show a lot of heart in battle, stomach the news, have wanderlust or basketball or calculus in our blood, spill out our guts in therapy, and are left breathless by the performance.

The similarity can be structural, as when we give someone a "tall" order. Or it can be functional, as when we lend someone an "ear."

It should be no surprise that sport has become an almost universal metaphor. The word "sport" itself, when applied to individuals, unveils a metaphoric connection. After all, what do we mean by being a "good" one? Someone who withstands adversity, who goes along with the program even though she may have not have initiated it, who can be humbled, even humiliated, who can lose, who can win, who's not all about me-me-me. The "poor" one, on the other hand, whines, makes excuses, is anything but cooperative, and chastises you for not getting better seats.

The reference to being a "Monday-morning quarterback" has become such a cliché that we hardly pay attention, but our indifference exemplifies how commonplace sport metaphors are. Business, investments, politics make use of them constantly, perhaps because of the essentially competitive nature of these activities. That psychology textbook with a picture of three runners reaching the tape is simply illustrating a common metaphor. Everything, even study, whatever the level of achievement, can be likened to a race.

In the last 48 hours alone, without being aware I had a special antenna out for them, I noticed the following:

The Oppenheimer Fund announces that you don't win a marathon in the first 100 yards. ("We believe in long-term investing, in staying in for the long haul," it feels obliged to add.) An Ameritrade ad has a group of marathoners at the start thinking independent thoughts ("Hey, I thought there'd be more women") with a caption implying its client stands out in a crowd. T. Rowe Price has us investors pictured as sailing through storms. In dismissing the efforts of one of the "apprentice" candidates, Martha Stewart hears the criticism that Ryan, in directing, producing and starring in a video, was "trying to pitch and catch at the same time," and the ball travels too fast to allow that.

Even the world inside the Beltway, lofty though it may (or may not) be, is not above the practice. Discussing possible Supreme Court nominees after Harriet Meiers withdrew, one commentator ventured the thought that the President was probably looking for an "intellectual heavyweight" and that so-and-so was the "odds-on favorite." These boxing and horse racing allusions sometimes join those in the more commonly used sports—baseball, basketball, football—to produce a linguistic trifecta (or triathlon, or triple-header). This president keeps getting the ball over the net; you think he's out, but he keeps getting back up. The Administration needed a slam-dunk and just when you think they're home safe, they get intercepted. Maybe they should have thrown a screen. As far as Fed tightening of interest rates goes, we're in the ninth inning.

Not only do I record all of this in a two-day period, I've begun to hear sport itself employing a different language to account for its otherwise esoteric vicissitudes. The metaphoree, in a word, has become the metaphorer. Strahan and Runyon—Giants defensive lineman and Eagles offensive tackle, respectively—playing the "game within the game" as advertised, are "doing a dance" as each thrust of the attacker is countered by a parry of the protector of the quarterback. Football as tango. Football as fencing. And yes, one sport can actually become a metaphor for another. Here's Patrick McEnroe describing Lindsay Davenport's failure to win when ahead at the 2005 Australian Open: "She hit the wall, like an endurance athlete." Are we going to crash into that wall whatever the course? Sorry, colleagues, no one has "writer's block" anymore, you just "hit the wall." No longer are marriages "on the rocks" (is that a sailing metaphor?), we just "hit the wall." Is there a time limit for marriages wherein the body can't take anymore, like the 20-mile glycogen-depletion barrier?[29]

Garry Kasparov, in announcing his retirement from chess last year because he wanted to broaden the scope of his interests, expressed his debt to the game of kings for having given him lessons for life.[30] Asked to be more specific, he gave the general and vague reply that it taught him to look at the big picture. Life apparently is a chess game, and you can get lost staring at only one small piece of it. I appreciate the metaphor, particularly as it may influence a person—a unique champion, as well—in the conduct of his life. But is finding one small similarity enough? Life is a tennis match. Life is a race or a fountain or a joke or a dice game or an obstacle course, and certainly no bed of roses. Running, it is often said, teaches one about ... having goals? But how much more is implied in that plethora of definitions? Recently, Dick Enberg, one of the commentators for CBS during the U.S. Open, liked the concept of the metaphor so much that he played with it on his "Behind the Lines" segment. The French Open is red *(terre battu)*, Wimbledon is white (think crisp British tennis whites, and for how long did they hold on to those white tennis balls?), and the U.S. Open is blue (even one of the court surfaces had been redone from green to blue). This was "blue-collar" tennis (not elite Wimbledon "white") in the mode of Jimmy Connors. Roddick got "blue" when he lost in the first round. And someone lying on the ground with cramps could have used Blue Cross.

Okay, but not quite. Or rather, not nearly enough. Be they likened to onions or roses, there's a lot more to metaphors

---

29 Anthropologist Helen Fischer seems to think so, citing four years as the critical time, the "four year itch" being the impetus to hit the road, in humans as well as some other primate species where the father sticks around, but only for so long. H. Fischer. *The Anatomy of Love.* New York: Norton; 1992.

30 G. Kasparov. "The Great Game." *Wall Street Journal:* March 14, 2005; p. A16.

than their skin color just as there's a lot more to selling corn flakes besides yellow packages (see Chapter Three). Are we ready now to decide what all of those definitions of the word "run" might mean?

As I've been indicating, I am provoked by there being more definitions for "run" than for any other word. In my modest Merriam–Webster's, there are 46 for the noun, 23 for the transitive verb, 27 for the intransitive verb. In the Webster's Third New International Dictionary, Unabridged of 2002, there are over three columns, 100 lines per column, before you get to the hyphenated ones ("run-down," "run-in") or composites ("runaway") or "running" participles ("running expenses," "running mate"). Are they all independent of one another? Is it an accident? Of course not. There's a similarity among all of them as well as to putting one foot rapidly in front of another.

I run down (go through) the list of meanings. Until I feel run down (exhausted). Then I recover and give it another run-through (trial, practice, rehearsal).

Why is the water, the Broadway show, the washing machine, the candidate running? What makes a running joke, a stocking run, a run of luck? We run into trouble, we run up our bills, we want to run with the fast crowd (and that doesn't usually mean getting to the starting line with the 5:30 group). We don't want to run ourselves into the ground. We run our eyes down the page and our ideas by our friends. We want to have the run of the mansion and not run up any costs and run with these ideas—not necessarily to run the whole show or run around the issues, but to give people a run for their money without using too many run-on sentences or having our discussion run into the early morning hours.

What are all these definitions about? Milton Erickson, a renowned therapist of slightly unusual bent who is fond of talking about and putting people into "trances" so that he may know something about the trance of running, commented that it's odd the hills run up and down when they don't move at all.[31] Erickson seems to have stumbled upon this peculiarity when attending to the different ways in which language is used, particularly cross-culturally. But my point is much more specific to running. The reason we have these many definitions and usages is that we employ the metaphor to show how so much of life is similar to running. So it's quite simple. Or is it? It's not just sport or running that substitutes for something else, but everything else (practically) that is a substitute for running.

The water running, the colors running, our noses running imply continual flow. We need a dam or a special detergent or an antihistamine to contain them, similar to those run-on sentences that run on and on because they're endless. We run up our bills. We don't know how it happened. Things got ahead of us. We couldn't control them. Running is heedless, unpredictable, blind and impetuous.

And, of course, fast. To "run with the fast crowd" means what? Simply to join in what moves quickly? No, it's to be with others in something exciting, compelling. The exact opposite, as it happens, from "run-of-the-mill," or ordinary. All runners are the same? Until we don our numbers and names. How, out of 37,000 runners, can our friends and family pick us out? Yes, 37,000 shirts and numbers, and 74,000 legs, and yet there we are, able to be found. And if we can distinguish ourselves from the run-of-the-mill, then we can do our best to be in charge, not to run blindly, not to have it be so unpredictable. Often described as boring (especially by those who abhor the treadmill), running is actually quite the opposite.

Ideally, though, running is smooth, a coordination of parts. The machine runs when it doesn't break down, when it doesn't stop and start, when it doesn't respond intermittently or halt-

---

31 J. Zeig. *A Teaching Seminar with Milton Erickson (Annual Progress in Child Psychiatry and Child Development).* Philadelphia, PA: Brunner/Mazel; 1980 (pp. 78, 173).

ingly. The expenditure of energy is minimal, perhaps optimal. It's efficient. But when the smoothness of the machine's operation is compromised—like when the washer in the laundromat gives you that "imbalanced" signal—it cannot continue with its task and stops. Running, therefore, implies balance.

These characteristics were supported by a brief talk I had with Deena Kastor recently. Kastor was the first American distance runner in so long to come home with an Olympic medal in the marathon, a bronze earned in the Athens games. She strained so hard in the following year's New York Marathon that she had to stop, and served as a commentator the next year. Kastor believes that the biggest secret of keeping on track is following a balanced life. Like so many spiritually minded runners, she finds inspiration in the Eastern philosophies that help keep her, shall we say, centered. She emphasizes the Japanese concept of *kaizen*—a key tenet of which is the cognizance and acceptance that you are part of a greater functioning whole. You keep going, yes, but with the understanding that someone else will always break your record; you put passion in, yes, but mix it with humility. And there is George Carlin, a self-confessed alcoholic for 67 years of his life, a man who is personally familiar with the imbalance of addiction, with much the same view. If we wish not to destroy nature and the environment, we had best cooperate rather than compete. When we see this approach applied to the process of running, we see it also before and afterward. Prepare by keeping balanced, not by excessive or obsessive concern. When we're through, we feel balanced and can better balance our lives. And, to turn the concept back in on itself, running is a prism through which we can address the different elements of that balance.

Why do we "run into each other;" why not simply say our paths crossed? Because the former phrase more accurately describes what actually happens. We're all on a course, but each person's avenue is unique. So running exemplifies both the universal and the particular.

When the show is having a good run, it may or may not be moving smoothly, but it is having a long and productive life. This "run" refers not to the process, but the product. So a good run implies longevity. Indeed, sometimes we use it for just that, to refer to a person's life; yes it's over, but he had a good run. When we run our eyes over the page, we're covering the course, we're not skipping around. We're not stopping deliberately; even though we seem to be looking for something, we're taking in the whole. Running is comprehensive. It's not hopping or jumping.

We run for office because it's an objective that not everyone can reach. It takes time and dedication. It's a project. We can't do it overnight. We don't sprint for office, or walk for office. So running, while it may seem something we can pick up anytime and continue, implies a dedication to a goal. It may be short range or long range, but it's certainly goal-directed. One of the most basic principles of sport psychology, particularly the psychology of running, is the importance of having goals. It's certainly similar to a business model, if those "apprentices" on Donald Trump's television show, talking endlessly about their objectives and "game plans," are any example. Have a goal in mind. Time or distance or frequency. Under four hours, six miles today, five times a week. Without it we tend to flounder, to be distracted by the rest of our lives. We don't want to wander for office. We want to run.

Of interest too is how goal setting is intrinsically connected to efficiency in general, and efficient running specifically. For where do you place your goal? Research on achievement motivation many years ago established that there were indeed differential characteristics in the high achiever not present in the low, specifically with respect to where they set their sights when goal-directed. Does the high achiever shoot for the moon, does he try the impossible, does he dream the impossible dream? Hardly. One who does that is more likely to be looking for an excuse for failure. ("Did I not make that shot? Oh, well, it was a pretty long shot.") Nor does the high achiever choose objectives that are too close. There, with success assured, success is not much. They choose—speaking of balance—moderate distances. The goal, if attained, therefore means something, but is not so out of reach as to be unobtainable.

If you are able to lift the bar—a frequently used sport metaphor these days—somewhat higher than your previous performance, you're on track for even greater success. What do you do when you fail? Raise it? Go for 3:30 if your previous attempt at 3:40 couldn't be reached? Run six times a week when five proved too much? That's how "failure avoidance" prevents "success achievement." No, you change your target time to 3:50, and shoot for four times per week. After success, raise it a bit. After failure, lower it. Sane, sensible, goal-directed behavior.

And what, then, is running around? When you give someone the "runaround" you're essentially not getting anywhere. Or, rather, you're not permitting him to get anywhere. But it's not the same when you're "running around." There, you're getting many places. You're not staying at one. You're not committed. So both "arounds" convey the idea that there's a lack of commitment to the enterprise.

But then the circle always represents the idea of coming back to the starting place. It's equally fascinating that while we run to cross the country, we also run in circles, on tracks, or (in Central Park) in loops. We get somewhere by getting nowhere. We come back to where we started. All that running (take the treadmill), and we get nowhere.

But at least that's better than running amok. In no discernible pattern. In all directions at once. Running, be it straight or around, has a calculus; slow or fast, it has a pace. It can be tracked. It's not random or chaotic.

So let's give people a run for their money. They paid, they deserve something, though we don't know necessarily what will happen or how they'll feel. Running is exciting. And yet we can feel run down. Running can't last forever. Much as we want it, our luck may run out. Running has an end. But if we can run on and run out, if it's endless and finite, then running ultimately is ambiguous. Which will it be? A run where I feel I can go forever, or a run where I want to stop as soon as I start?

Ultimately this will run its course. We can't predict. We have to wait. Not everything's controllable, particularly running.

But let me emphasize why, psychologically, the metaphor is so all-important. One of Freud's major contributions to our understanding of how to view therapy was the concept of transference. The therapeutic situation, the relationship to the analyst, is similar to and perhaps a reflection of situations or relationships in the patient's life. It's why nothing in psychoanalytic psychotherapy is excluded. If you want to comment on the therapist's wall hangings, go ahead. Is that about what was (is) hanging over your head since childhood? Or let's say, without being quite that metaphorically transferential or transferentially metaphoric, you get angry at your therapist for not saying something when you ask him a question. At whom are you really angry? A parent who didn't answer you? Of course, this is simplistic Freud, but it's meant to be. One situation reflects another.

But an appreciation of transference (and there are even those who take it to the extreme—a patient will enact in her first session the important themes of her life, they say) leads to discovering its application to other walks (or runs) of life. If we learn how we approach our boss or librarian or significant other, we may indeed learn about ourselves. Of course there may be differences, but these also can have similarities. Perhaps you approach people behind desks or behind glasses or behind glass doors differently from those … what? In front?

Without barriers? Do you see them as barriers? Life is indeed a tennis match, and not just in Woody Allen's sense in *Match Point,* that luck determines success or failure. Your tennis game is a metaphor for your personality, reflected in the way you rush or don't rush the net, whether you come from behind, whether you go for broke.

There is a subgroup of the American Psychological Division of Sport Psychologists known as Running Psychologists. When I first heard of them, it sounded like a joke. Psychologists who run? Psychologists who treat runners? Psychologists who run with their patients and then treat them? Well, all the above. They were, some of them, actually out there running with patients, then coming in to the office to discuss what they'd seen. Did they start out slow and then pick up? Did they get close to the finish line and then stop? Did they underestimate or overestimate their ability, say they're not competing and then compete zealously, talk nonstop, complain, distort (how much they ran, for example), manipulate (tell you it's not something they care about or do well, and then ferociously attack the course)? You think you can leave your personality behind when you head out for the track? Quite the contrary. Everything we do is readable from the way we do it, should we have a good reader. It may sound a little more Billy Crystal than Freud (*Analyze This, Analyze That*) to leave the couch behind and run or be dragged out into the mob scene, but Freud was actually a lot less "Freudian" than many of his disciples. He did in fact, if not make house calls, at least occasionally see patients at work, at play, *in situ, en famille.*

Malcolm Gladwell in *Blink* affirms the metaphoric principle.[32] A couple's first meeting is a snapshot of their relationship. Does she expect him to take care of things? Does he expect her to be deferential, social, inquisitive, dominating, ambitious, organized, sexually provocative? Broaden the

32 M. Gladwell. *Blink.* New York: Little, Brown & Co.; 2005 (p. 63).

scene and you will witness the same. What goes on in X, that first date, is a microcosm of what goes in Y, their life together. In former Arkansas Governor and now presidential hopeful Mike Huckabee's account, the same point is implicit.[33] His list of life lessons to get himself in better shape has as much to do with other areas as it does with dieting and exercise. Stop procrastinating, make a little list of changes, change the reward system, set a specific time, share it with others, and just put one foot in front of the other. He told me in person that one way he got through those 26 miles (he ran his first marathon at age 49) was to do each one for a separate person in his head (mile 22 for Aunt Doris, 23 for his son, and so on). When you're thinking of quitting any activity that you know you really want to stick with, would that not be a way of getting through?

It may be useful to summarize some of these metaphoric points under the heading, "Lessons for Life." Since I'm implying that much of what I say here is intended to mean just that, it may also be redundant. But sometimes you need to cover the same ground to make sure you haven't missed something. So let me run it by you to make sure it doesn't run by us.

We have goals, but we shouldn't set them too high. We can adjust goals, and once we have them it's less likely we'll get distracted. It's good to anticipate and to practice. Where are the runners bunching, at which exit do I get off, on what streets can I walk fast without hitting lights, the obvious applications. But are the metaphoric implications quite so obvious? Do I want to run into people or do I want to go around them? Have I never considered the latter until I started running? Did I think it too, what, political? Unmasculine? Until I realized I

33 M. Huckabee. *Quit Digging Your Grave with a Knife and Fork: A 12-Step Program to End Bad Habits and Begin a Healthy Lifestyle.* New York: Center Street; 2005.

really was hurting myself by running into them?

Something as mundane as eating, or as complicated as eating on the run, serves the runner well. (I know I've distanced myself from any omega-3 knowledge, but I must say that flaxseed, walnuts and kale are not bad things for the arteries to know about after all; maybe they're easier to come by than those miles.) Know yourself and adjust accordingly. Are you too easy on yourself? Then push. Are you too hard? Then relax. If I'm delayed by traffic and won't find it easy to do my few miles in the evening, and am still planning to do the long run of eighteen tomorrow, because while I always did it on Sunday, it couldn't be done on this Sunday, so I had to postpone it a day—then, good. Give yourself a break. I've been going out there when time was short, squeezing in some miles between patients, and yes, it feels good to have done it. I've even been asked by some, when the sweat was still beading on my brow and I'd only just peeled my white socks to reveal the black underneath, whether I'd been running. But be wary of giving yourself too many breaks. Yes, I'm tired, didn't get enough sleep, am hung over, have a blister, have no desire, have too much work, and if I leave it for the end of the day, the excuses will abound and the motivation will be less.

We don't want to run out of steam. You will if you start too fast. You think you'll be ahead of the game and keep something in reserve, but in reality you'll tire too quickly. The lesson from this is to modulate your level of excitement and see how this applies to other activities.

Keep in mind, though, that maximum performance occurs at moderate levels of anxiety. Too much and you become paralyzed, or get the yips before you putt. You're tongue-tied, stage-frightened, hyperventilating at the bottom of a hill or just too embarrassed to try moving up to a faster training group. On the other hand, if you experience no stress, if you're not somewhat "psyched up" before the race, if your emotional cardiogram is completely flat, it's hard to get up for anything. You might not want to emulate those football behemoths chest-thumping before the game, but moderate levels of excitement, even dread, are optimal.

And this applies to other emotions as well. Stop pushing yourself, stop being obsessive, stop demanding you go out there every day and constantly increase your level of performance. Okay, but if you feel guilty you haven't had your workout for the day, that guilt is a form of incentive. It's not altogether bad. In fact, while I hardly felt guilt not running the week after the marathon, had I stopped entirely (a thought which certainly occurred to me), I would have felt guilty. Not just about the expected weight gain, but about having abandoned an activity with which I had developed a relationship, if not quite a loving one. We were now acquainted. I had followed lots of guidelines, though I hadn't quite finished the task. Indeed, I might never.

But guilt because you haven't exceeded your fellow runners' or parents' or whomever's expectation is not only inappropriate, it can be dangerous. I have one patient who was so depressed she couldn't be the good girl in her mother's eyes and forsake all earthly pleasures (or at least sexual ones), that she became suicidal. And of course, the anorexic is so guilty she's indulged in any appetite, she must avoid satisfying it at all costs. But one of the functions of the superego is to do just that, to remind us when we eat too much ice cream or sleep through our classes that we're doing ourselves ultimate harm, even if it feels good in the short run.

There is often a similarly confusing amount of information on the emotion of anger. On the one hand it gets you in trouble, so you must learn how to control it. On the other, suppressing it leads to depression, ulcers, or explosive acting out, so express it. The solution is relatively easy to theorize, if sometimes hard to enact. Talk about it and be done with it.

Immediately, without violence, and swiftly. Like a parent's bark, it will be disciplinary to the child and effective. I've often noticed that there are some athletes (John McEnroe, prime example) who seem to feed on their anger, who seem to play better when they can express all that's inside of them. I think it's true even of those who resemble him the least. When Andre Agassi played a marvelous point against Rafael Nadal in 2005 and undid some of his previous errors, he found himself, the "Zen master," according to Barbra Streisand's description years earlier, unable to express his anger at his opponent for taking too long to get ready for the next point. He petulantly said something to the umpire about playing to "his pace," but since Nadal was within his rights to towel off and take 30 seconds, Agassi, trying to prove he was more fit than this opponent half his age, just stewed. And promptly double-faulted, then made an uncharacteristic error, lost his edge, the third set and the match. When Bjorn Borg got a bad line call in the first set tie-breaker—and his last big match—against McEnroe in the 1981 U.S. Open, he merely hesitated, stared and quit the game when he lost the match. And the turning point in Ivan Lendl's career? Lendl, who went on to be Number One, a finalist in eight consecutive U.S. Opens, he who had previously always failed in the clutch or the big one? I remember it well. It was the fourth set of the French Open against McEnroe in 1984. McEnroe had won the first two and was on his way to an unprecedented winning year. But he lost this one, because he muttered something after Lendl hit a big shot, something like you lucky f***. And Lendl, instead of ignoring it, came to the net and challenged him. For once, McEnroe's brattiness was being called. Lendl let him have it and McEnroe tucked his tail between his legs and lost.

I've often barked when pedestrians cut me off in Central Park, oblivious to all but their partners and destination, like someone deliberately sticking out his foot to trip me. And generally, I've noted, my breathing gets better. It's the theory behind some therapies and therapy techniques. Hit the pillow, not your partner. Manage your anger, but recognize it first as a means of controlling it. Express it verbally, not physically. It's there and often justified. When I somewhat wryly referred to myself in Chapter One as an angry New Yorker, what I was really suggesting was that if you don't have egrets and ospreys in your running path but leashes and double strollers, you don't have to be blinded by rage—you can use it. It is, like all the emotions, an energy source. Don't turn it off. The pipes might explode.

And therein lies another point about anger. I've often noted how accepting runners are. In fact, I can't think of a more cooperative group than the Running Psychologists I've become part of relatively recently. But it was more than cooperating with a fellow researcher. They genuinely seemed much more open to having fun, to working, to being gracious. But if a runner is more accepting—of the errant pedestrian, for example—something is definitively being suppressed. I recall that when London had its underground bombing experience in 2005, they went about their business, as is the Brits' wont, with a stiff upper lip and seemingly undeterred. But were they manifesting extreme tolerance or simply suppressing their feelings out of a need to be in control, to seem to be in control, not to let the terrorists have the upper hand? Beware of seeming calmness; it not only augurs of the storm, but masks the one brewing underneath.

While basically a solitary activity (okay, "sport"), running can make you a bit more sensitive to other people as well. I haven't yet told some of my couples in therapy to run together, but I'm sure it's coming, and others I know have. For one thing, it teaches you that very few people are on exactly the same pace. To do that, they must adjust, sometimes radically. Bless my kids for going out with me and doing some of those training runs, but they had to hold back considerably to run side by side with me and with each other. Maybe it helped them too. Not to improve their speed, but to do something they thought worth-while, to encourage and assist the old man.[34] People travel this world at their own pace. Perhaps it's obvious, but you wouldn't think so judging from the way we demand that others see or react to our needs. We're not all ticker-tape-watching day traders, moving in or out in nanoseconds or losing the oppor-tunity. In fact, it might be well for that group—indeed, for all of us—to pause and get a slightly slower and more distant and broader perspective on those up- and downticks.

There are also fundamental differences in peoples' individ-ual reactions to pain. While compromising ones wants or needs seems to be a fundamental ingredient for relationship-survival, this dimension is rarely attended to with enough care. I'll have more to say on this later, but suffice it to note at this point that had I known this earlier in relation to some of my own significant others, we might have stuck it out a bit longer before diverging onto our separate paths.

Unlike golf or scuba diving or even tennis, running does not take much equipment. There are some hardy old-timers, in fact, who take pride in their pre-"running shoes" and "Coolmax" days when a pair of gym shoes and Keds were more than sufficient. So it's ironic that running has actually made me more conscious of physical preparation. Maybe I wasn't paying enough attention to those women (mother, sister, grandmother) up with whom I grew, or maybe it's simply a "guy thing," but the first person I learned of who placed her clothes for the next day out the night before (actually it was a

---

34 Not nearly the impetus provided by a five-year-old in Prospect Park, pink ribbons around her dreadlocks as she dismounted her pink-wheeled bicycle in the middle of the hill, staring incredulously at me huffing and puffing, and shouted, "C'mon, old man, you can do it." I glared and promptly doubled my pace until I was well out of her sight.

patient of mine, and a true obsessive) amazed me, since I couldn't imagine having the time or energy to do any such thing. I usually finish tying my shoes or putting on a tie in elevators and subways. What better use for that static time? But now? After a marathon where two weeks before I was wondering about my shirt options—long-sleeved, short-sleeved, body shirt, one, two, three layers, sweatpants, shorts—making sure they were all clean and ready to go before even getting to the power bars, bananas, bagels, Gatorade, safety pins, toilet-paper rolls, behaving as if I was the supply sergeant preparing for a six-month expedition from the South Pole to the Sahara, I now have been known actually to think about what I'm going to wear Saturday night to the ball.

No dimension seems more related to running than time. It takes time. We all pay attention to our time, no matter what the sages say about not letting it be—particularly at your first marathon—an overwhelming consideration. Everyone rushes over to those sheets that get posted on the fences at the end of most races to see how he or she did. But there are other aspects of time that get highlighted through running. Schedules, to be sure, but I'm thinking of whether —and if so, how—one's perspective on time changes. How much time do we in fact spend wondering how to use time effectively? How many errands do we not go on because they will take 45 minutes of our time just to travel each way, and it's not worth it? Having spent so many hours—two, three, four, and now nearly five at a clip—doing nothing but running (whatever else was going on in my head), traveling from one spot back to the same spot, very little of what I want to do seems not worth the time. I have much the same take on distance. I can now go by foot anywhere, it seems (except maybe Katmandu); certainly to Brooklyn if there's a black-out, as there was just before I started my running escapade. And how much time then was spent trying to figure out a five-bus route to get a stranded friend home? I stare in amazement at people getting off a bus at Third Avenue that they've boarded at First. In fact, the only concession I could conceive of making to buses these days is that, after running the 26.2, I considered taking one to the after-party. But not only did it seem superfluous, not many were running anyway. So maybe that's the lesson … when people run, buses don't. Once you've run, you rarely need them.

Running is an intense activity. Physical, but also mental (as I'm trying to demonstrate). It is thus necessary to rest. Give yourself that time and option, particularly you type-A sorts. God ran for six days and saw it was good. Then He tapered.

Many have said this and that brings up a related point: that I can actually learn from people. It was, as you may remember, one of my handicaps when I started. I prefer going my own way. It takes a lot for me to be curious enough about anything to follow another's lead. Granted, I've had my share of education, but I've probably taken no more than half a dozen classes in the last 30 years, and I can't tell you if I learned anything from any of them. But I've read a little and attended a running clinic or two. Even given one (or two). And while many of these running gurus seem a little simplistic or single-minded or pedantic or narcissistic (not unlike the majority of "experts" I've encountered elsewhere), I have actually found myself copying down and heeding some of their advice and, particularly before the marathon, last-minute hints and recipes. I started cooking kale. And looking for flax. And yes, in the last week, paying attention to hydration. I haven't yet enrolled for hot-tub yoga and swing dancing, but who knows? I may have discovered my inner optimist.

And yes, I run into another result of my watching myself on the track. Always keep in mind the opposite. As I mentioned earlier, the antidote for a strict regimen is relaxing the reins or schedule a bit. The plan is important but not etched in stone. I forgave myself for skipping Sunday and it was good. Monday came.

Am I running out of gas? Hardly, but yes, so what does it mean? That ultimately, running implies being fueled. And not just with alpha-6 or omega-3 or carbs. With the will to continue. Like life itself.

It does appear that there's some evidence that, apart from all the physical conditions we're used to, the mind plays a part in our longevity as well. More people die in the trimester following their birthday than that preceding it. It appears that we can, to a degree, last when we're looking forward. The growth of "health psychology" and the pairing of religion and psychology, the emphasis on how mental attitudes or depression affect the growth of cancer, all lend credence to this idea. *The New England Journal of Medicine* reports that of those people who have heart attacks, there is a four-time greater fatality rate when the person is depressed. And in controlled experiments, those who are depressed suffer heart attacks four times as frequently. To a degree we do, as the football commentators are forever observing toward the end of the season, control our own destiny. We indeed may run out of gas, before we sputter and stall.

And yet, to run our course, there is only so much we can do to keep the motor running. Eat well and exercise and have a healthy, positive attitude, to be sure. But we're not totally in control. Collapsing buildings and tsunamis and terrorists can get us, no matter how cautious and prudent we are. Life, too, runs its course.

5

Running with the Fast (and Slow) Crowd— Social Facilitation

It was the last three-and-a-half miles of what was amusingly called a race but, as you know by now, was my first marathon. And my last. When it was done, I hadn't done so badly, I had finished, I had survived, I had done so in the same week I had started, I had pulled or strained or contorted nothing, and I had surmounted the wall despite my children's worrying to such an extent that they were greeting and jogging with me at mile 20 and 21 and 22. I hadn't fallen on the cups or the newly prepared and presented Sponge-Bob designer sponges, though it took a high-stepping jig to avoid them. I was going to make it in respectable time if not record time, at least for my age group (actually finishing, if barely, in the first half of my old-fogy section). I was passing people left and right, some who were actually walking those last six miles, and others who were running but clearly with some difficulty. I didn't know them and that was good, because I had remembered from a training run that beginning to talk to someone on pace early left me feeling somewhat guilty when I left him in the dust later.

And then the crowd along Fifth Avenue and in the park was so close they could be touched. We were exchanging not just waves but high-fives, and they were shouting "Let's go Ethan," "Show us what you've got, Ethan," "Looking good, Ethan," and what had seemingly been such a surprise and inspiration earlier now seemed a bit forced and jaded. It gave me something, but it also took something away. I was getting distracted. Enough already. Use their energy? Yes, it was nice, but it was also dangerously close to overload. I could blow a fuse.

And long after the race was run, I heard this sentiment from others long after their races had been run. Some of us, without really knowing it, put great stock in our ability to concentrate, whether it was on the road or the other runners or the time (clocks clearly visible at every mile), to block out all the reasons why this is crazy. And now, if I looked over and saw who was cheering, I'd be reminded too much of what I was doing, as well as wondering if I knew them and whether I could go out with them later and have a beer or sex. And once I started doing that, I was not just plodding along, I was plotting along.

So what's this about social facilitation? In 1897 Triplett discovered that bikers went faster with other riders around them—personal-best times are often achieved in races where others surpass their own fastest times.[35] We get inspired by others doing the same task or watching us do it, or we're so competitive that our juices flow when we get the opportunity to have others with us, spurring us on. I had remembered this from a colleague of mine who I'd accidentally learned had

---

35 G. Allport, "The Historical Background of Modern Social Psychology." In: G. Lindzey and E. Aronson, eds. *The Handbook of Social Psychology, 2nd ed.* Reading, MA: Addison-Wesley; 1968 (pp. 64–65).

done the marathon 25 years earlier. He hit the wall at the 19th mile, and he and his fireman partner "pulled each other through." They talked. They joked. They forgot their pain. Or is the crowd effect due to something else, that we don't dare disappoint others once we've gone out on the limb and said we intend to do it? In fact, that's a good incentive to run—tell people you're doing it. Tell them you're writing a book. What I'm writing? No, that will dissipate my energy. But *that* I'm writing yes, now I must do it.

And over the years, it's been a source of investigation and some satisfaction. We get better in the presence of others. Zajonc modified it somewhat to say we did when we were over the hump—that is, if you were "good" you got better but if you were "bad" you got worse.[36] And that would explain some things, like why some rose to heights never before experienced when the crowd was with them while others faltered, became dumbstruck, forgot their lines, stumbled over their jokes, tripped on the ice. And perhaps it also accounts for the annoyance I would feel when others, alleged supporters, minimized the extent of the job. First, there are those who have done it before. Oh, you've run ten, then the marathon's no problem. Oh, you've run twenty, well then it surely won't be a problem. So it's never a problem—except when it's a problem. And even worse are the finishers ahead of you, be it a 5k or a half-marathon, who walk back over the course shouting the "encouraging" words that you're almost there. I remember it distinctly at the end of my first half-marathon in Brooklyn, wondering why that finish line wasn't where it was supposed to be since all the ones coming down the hill were telling us laggards the goal was just ahead. That last 0.1 of the 13.1 was interminable. You think 26.2 is no problem once you've done 20? It's just under 25 percent of a problem. To you, it's not because

---

36 R. Zajonc. "Social Facilitation." In: H. Lindgren, ed. *Contemporary Research in Social Psychology.* New York: John Wiley & Sons; 1969 (p. 100).

you've done it. To you, it's almost over because it is over. To you, who've stood up and delivered your sermon or comedy routine to millions on television, you're inspired, but to us behind who haven't, we're going to get worse.

But even more to the point, Zajonc's theory, well founded in some laboratories, couldn't hold up even by everyday standards. After all, it was Laurence Olivier, hardly a novice, who got such stage fright at the thought of performing before an audience each night that he had to throw up every time he performed. It was five-time medal winner Eric Heiden who fell in the Olympics, not once but twice. It couldn't be as simple as the good got better, etc. The good also suffered. Is it then a blind choice between social facilitation and social inhibition?

So there we have it. At a premarathon lecture the previous year (yes, ever since I wanted to see my kids at the finish line, I'd made myself the marathon shrink for the New York Road Runners and been giving talks on Visualization and Psychological Preparation), I was discussing this idea of social facilitation and why it was such a good idea to wear your number, if not on your sleeve, then clearly on your shirt. A young woman in the back interrupted with a question, wondering whether this was necessarily advisable. She had observed that when she ran, she was in her own world and it was actually disconcerting if others called out to her. She was presciently alerting me to what I've indicated I experienced.

Yes, I liked it, as they sang in the overture to *Cheers,* when someone knew my name. Yes, it felt, as one of my sons said when he first experienced it, as if it were a parade just for him, but I also worried about it. When my kids cheered seeing me at the six-mile mark, then 14, then 18, then 21, I indeed loved it because I knew they meant it and were out there to give what support they could (particularly since somewhere deep down they must have had the fear that I might not make it out of the starting gate, much less past the "wall" where they, too, had faltered and lost time in the half-dozen marathons they'd done between them), from bananas to bellowing cheers. But from the strangers, I began to experience something else— enough already, you're showboating, you're insincere.

And so there's a lesson about support and crowds. Come out, but don't overdo it. We're too smart to think that you're always going to be there, through thick and thin, unless you love us (and even then, how often does it indeed wear thin)?

And we can add another factor to the social psychology mix. A primary motive for why people continue and don't continue is the principle of shame or embarrassment. A leader in the field of sport psychology, Fran Pirozzolo, an advisor to the Houston Texans football team who has worked extensively with golfers, introduced the idea of deliberately missing shots, purposely shanking them, so you'll get used to the experience.[37] Inoculate yourself, so the theory goes, as a way of coping with strange or unfamiliar circumstances.

The implicit assumption here is that one of the reasons people fail when competing or performing is not because they make a mistake, but because of what happens afterwards. I hypothesized in my exploration of tennis that extroverts had to win early in matches, because if they fell behind they'd be obliged to get out of there, the arena in which they were exposed, quickly. They couldn't stand to look bad. Whether a result of tension, or distraction, you're no longer concentrating as much on the ball if you're worried about the audience or reflecting on your last mistake. So it follows that when someone makes a mistake, he will tend to make another. One error begets a second.

Therefore, to forestall or eliminate this pattern, make the mistake deliberately, early, in practice. Now should it happen

---

37 B. Wysocki, Jr. "It's a Living." *Wall Street Journal,* September 20, 2005; p. B1, 4.

in real life—that is, when the chips are down and the tournament has begun—it will not appear or even be so extraordinary to you. It will be familiar. You will have encountered it before, you may even be able to shrug or laugh it off, and the devastating roller coaster of mistakes will be less likely to occur.

Other people provide us a forum to excel, but also one in which to judge us failures. Shame is a reflection of the latter—we haven't been able to overcome a basic feeling of inadequacy which is present when others are present. This is part of our socialization process. We learn to adapt by suspending our own vulgar practices, whether it's defecating in public, whenever or wherever we want, or eating without the proper utensils, and thus the ever-continuing process of socialization begins. But this means we really are acting unnaturally in the presence of others, suspending our normal behavior patterns, and resenting on some level that we can't revel in or grovel in our own solitary and unexamined practices. Is the unexamined life not worth living? Indeed, as we rise up the evolutionary ladder and become philosophical and ethical and kind. But what of the overexamined life, as anyone who dates a psychologist will attest? I've often heard a prospective companion murmur over the first drink, "Are you going to analyze me too?" Leave me alone, let me do my own thing, stop watching, a first principle and protest of the human organism.

6

The Normal Run of Things— Personality Types

Let me assure you from the outset that I give as much credence to the DSM's (Diagnostic and Statistical Manual) list of psychiatric or psychological disorders as I do to the belief that there's one normal way of cooking, eating, dressing, hitting a tennis ball, … or running. Yes, there is doubtless some value in recognizing the truly pathological, like the schizophrenic, because then he can be helped or removed from danger to himself or others. And yes, true attention-deficit disorder might be something for which to look out, particularly if you're a parent (but not to the extent it seems to have become an epidemic recently, having been contracted by the enterprisingly manipulative as a means of getting extra time on standardized tests). But this catalog now has more entries than the public library's list of discontinued periodicals and, despite its continual updating, may be about as useful.

Organized by psychiatrists and psychologists in emulation of the medical model of characterizing disease, it is used primarily these days to convince insurance companies that what you're seeing in a psychological patient is indeed "real" and describable by "specific behavioral descriptors" that address "clinical information that impact treatment" such as "symptom progression, concomitant issues, and effectiveness of current strategies," so when they conduct their "utilization review" and "grievance handling" and "external review" and "quality assurance" and "dispute resolution" and "peer review," they will exhaust everyone except the lawyers from going further to question their policies.

If we know something about characterizing what appear to be abnormalities because they reflect cognitive, emotional or behavioral components of the human psyche, it's because we have a rough idea of what's "normal," and hence are alert to thought disturbances, emotional disturbances, or behavioral disturbances. If indeed you think you see ghosts or hear voices telling you to mount the Empire State Building naked or—dare we say it these days?—strap a belt loaded with bb shot and other explosive particles into the lobby of a hotel or pizza parlor, then you have a serious problem with reality. If you find yourself absolutely enraged when someone steps off a curb waiting for a light or passes you quite legally on a highway, then you have a problem with controlling your feelings. If you're then inclined to follow this person for twenty miles until you cut him off or run into him or tell him off, you have a problem modulating your behavior and separating it from the feelings that produced it. It was to Freud's credit that he demonstrated his early patients diagnosed with "hysteria"—a loss of control of part of the body manifesting as twitching, coughing, itching, and even paralysis, blindness, or deafness, and so called because the majority of doctors believed that such individuals were either shamming or imagining their symptoms since they could find nothing physically wrong with them—were actually suffering from something quite real. And by reasoning that if it's real and not physical, then it must be psychological, and that otherwise quite normal people in the mainstream of society could develop these symptoms, he helped contribute to the depathologizing of "abnormality." The line between normal and abnormal, in other words, is quite thin, and most of his attention—to our *lapsus linguae,* our everyday forgetting, our misplacing of objects, our calling people by the wrong name—showed us how common were such errors (described as "The Psychopathology"—strong word—"of Everyday Life"). He was finding the abnormal in the otherwise quite normal, in other words. And similarly, by having us understand what the roots of serious pathology might be—how paranoia or obsessive compulsiveness or even schizophrenia might arise from the everyday world of relationships, even, as we know too well, toilet training—he was finding the normal in the abnormal. There, but for the grace of a mother's love or a quite restrained reaction to my tantrum or not being left alone with my fantasies of ghosts, go I.

So when I call these normal and abnormal behaviors, I should really refer to them with quotes. Psychologists have for some time sought to identify personality types—and we can certainly see them exemplified in the sport arena—but I'm introducing the concept of "abnormality" because I also believe that extreme behaviors (like running supermarathons or just plain marathons, or running every day or almost every day or sacrificing one's other activities, even one's life, to these things) come from something that can be identified as pathological. And if you listen to some medical experts, running itself is absolutely crazy. You can damage so many vital parts of yourself, only lunatics would think of doing this. One runner I knew was actually told by her gynecologist to stop, since it's apparently possible to loosen or dislodge your uterus and cause it to fall.

There is little denying that running can be addictive. And it's true that there's a type of addictive personality that does himself and others little harm, and may even be spurred on to do valuable work. As the air waves commemorated Mozart's 250th birthday, one was reminded that many great artists must owe at least some portion of their greatness to their addiction. But it is also clear that something is not right about such addiction. True addiction, by any definition, is hard to stop. You don't just enjoy sex or alcohol or running—you HAVE TO HAVE IT. Is it any wonder that it's a commonplace to think of artists as "mad?"

Both "normal" and "abnormal" types emerge, to the psychoanalyst, from less-than-optimal treatment in the early years. While we sophisticates raise our eyebrows should anyone take Freudian discussion of "oral tendencies" or "unresolved Oedipal complexes" too literally any more, it is also evident that many concepts are part of our everyday usage and vocabulary (I've heard third-graders refer to their overly conscientious classmate as being "so-o-o anal"). And many a therapist will not hesitate in relying on them for his interpretation of characterological behavior, as exemplified in the overly generous person who seeks to please others, in the overly dependent person who cannot initiate activities herself, in the overly exhibitionist person who enjoys an activity only when others applaud his efforts rather than deriving satisfaction from the doing. It can be of interest to take any index of the personality—say, as we'll do in the discussion of "motivational" differences in runners—and trace it to such origins. Is my own refusal to take medical advice, for example, an anal reaction to being told to sit down, stop complaining and do as I'm told?

In later theory, personality development is determined not so much by primitive feelings (pursuit of the bottle, fascination with what distinguishes a boy from a girl), but by considerations that are more social. Freud's student and colleague, Carl Jung, introduced the now-familiar "extrovert" and "introvert" types that are characterized by their relationship to the outer world.[38] What distinguishes the two is not so much a matter of one being more socially minded than the other, as common parlance would have us believe, as it is finding the source of one's being outside of oneself or inside. Where does the extrovert go when he's in a crisis or, more correctly put, toward whom does he turn ("vert" meaning turn)? He turns to others. He gets on the telephone. What does the introvert do when faced with a crisis? Locks himself in his room and unplugs the phone.

Incidentally, has the cell-phone revolution not brought home with a vengeance how needy so many of us are to hear from others? You think high-tech is simply providing us a greater level of communication? Then you must be a sales rep for Nokia or Motorola or Ericsson. You think valuable, real-time text-message information is what's being instantaneously delivered? (Destined for 77th Street, the caller announces, "Hi, I'm on 76th Street, I'm on my way, I'll be there in six minutes, are we still on?") No, neediness, an inability to be alone, to rely on oneself (extroverted characteristics), to commit to that appointment without constant reaffirmation is what's being revealed. My patients—don't get me started!—do not need to check in or "confirm" that we're still on. We're confirmed when we make the appointment, even—*mirabile dictu*—one that was made two weeks ago.

And it's not just in response to crises that we see the difference. Everything from sensitivity to distraction to responding to outer stimuli can be involved. The introvert cannot stand the whisper in the library, the ticking of the clock, the dripping of the faucet. He is too attuned to the disruption that

---

38 C. Jung, G. Adler, R. F. C. Hull. *Psychological Types.* Princeton, NJ: Princeton Univ. Press; 1976 (pp. 4, 6).

these conditions cause in his own inner-wrapped world. Whereas the extrovert loves to study to the tune of rap music or feels most comfortable in the crowded, noisy, strobe-lit discotheque (do they still exist?), club or bar.

Focusing on this early distinction of types works particularly well in running, where so much seems to depend on or relate to this dimension of the inner and outer. What do you think of when you run? On what are you focused? Do you see the birds and the trees, or do you think of the birds and the bees? Do you count how many miles you've logged, or how many moving feet you've passed?

Some research on the subject distinguishes associators from dissociators; and if we compound these with Jungian-style focusing, we arrive at four types:[39]

The first are the external associators, who pay attention to outer stimuli having to do with racing or the run—other runners, the time, the road, the water stations, the spectators. In the case of my marathon, I have to admit that for the first time in any run, I became conscious, or more conscious, of all these, since it would seem you have to. No, I take that back; you have to at certain points. When trying to get around a corner with half a dozen others who were cutting the tangent, it was important to pay attention to them and make adjustments accordingly so as not to be disrupted (admittedly I saw no one fall, but that wasn't because of the generosity of the group with which I was bumping elbows). When sprinting down those last few miles in Central Park, I was not just slapping hands with some spectators, but alert to who was a bit over the line so as not to see my marathon end in a Derek Jeter-like tumble, following a foul ball into the stand; had I hit ground, I'm sure it would have taken a forklift to get me back up. The grounds at the water sta-

---

39 W. Morgan. "Hypnosis in Sport and Exercise Psychology." In: J. Van Raalte and B. Brewer, eds. *Exploring Sport and Exercise Psychology.* Washington, D.C.: APA; 1996 (p. 123).

tions, particularly the later ones, were so strewn with cups and liquid that it was practically impossible not to find your shoes and socks immersed. The worst areas were those with the sponges that so littered the course one had to high-step through and around them as if it were an army obstacle course. I was frankly amazed not to see runners sucked in by them and tumbling like bowling pins for a quarter mile after each station.

So it serves a marathoner well to watch where he's going, and that would seem to be one of the things that external associators are doing. I wish the same were true of sidewalk amblers, cell-phone obsessive or not, who are looking anywhere but straight ahead. But the attention to other parts of race-related external events is also because it gives you a lift. Attention to time clocks helps regulate your inner one. And attention to crowds, particularly when they're calling your name (I had mine pinned above my number), did provide some inspiration before, as I said earlier, it began to pall. So did other "runners," many of whom were walking (some were doing this pretty much from the start, apparently as a kind of strategy, since I could hear from their cell phones that they were keeping track of the location of some of their friends; but others were doing it at various strategic points, particularly up every bridge), and from whom I derived a perverse kind of satisfaction because I wasn't. I was still running. And yes, all those runners that I somehow passed those last couple of miles helped. In fact, even the faster ones at that point were an inspiration, because I could imagine tracking some down, or at least running their pace for a few strides in the belief that I could either catch them or pick it up a bit and improve my time. And as I write this, I realize that I was not aware of how many things I was aware of in that outer world until I started recapturing it. I can now recall what must have been registered so fast that I couldn't keep track of it on the actual track. It was indeed, as Malcom Gladwell would have it, a "blink."

Then there are the external dissociators. They essentially practice a form of distraction, one that I rarely found myself using during practice runs or other races. They pay attention to what doesn't have to do with the race: the trees, the clouds (well, actually, if you're looking at clouds to see if they're lifting or letting the sun through, that's probably race connected). I was put on alert for this race that it would be hot, that runners would be dropping—as indeed they did in past races at the later mile points—with cramps or fatigue. So when the day began overcast it was a blessing, and it wasn't until much later that we were coming into the sun and feeling more of what turned out to be a 70-degree and 97-percent-humidity day. Nevertheless, clouds and birds and buildings and the multifarious, overly famous multinational groups and neighborhoods of this city were certainly there on which to be focused or from which to be distracted, and I tried also, with some minimal attention, to use them. But rather than enjoying the groups of Chasidim staring at us in disbelief in Williamsburg, I found myself using my Yiddish to chastise the woman with her stroller who tried to scurry, not altogether successfully, across the street in front of us. And in Bedford–Stuyvesant, when suddenly the empty lots and garages dotted a landscape with considerably fewer people, I found myself annoyed that our cheerleaders were so much less in evidence and started blaming the apathetic few playing cards and dominoes on sidewalk tables for not cheering us on and remaining relatively oblivious to the 37,000 runners passing. Or were they just bored, now that the leaders had long since passed and it was the masses' turn? But the ability to take it all in, even that which was irrelevant to the race, seemed to help.

And then soon, another turn around Lafayette, and it was hard to dissociate because the helpful crowds were back, handing out everything from water to hard candies to what looked like icicles (I never got a chance to grab one and would have been too scared to put anything strange into my mouth), but still I was thanking them and trying to request a paper towel of a seven-year-old benefactor, who unfortunately was having more demands made of her than she could fulfill quickly enough. And throughout it all, in this amazing city known not just for its cooperative hordes, or this rude, callous, uncaring city where crime always looms, there was not one incident of arrogance or vandalism, not one attempt to throw us off stride in some adolescent and cruel manner. Were the mayor and police so efficient, or was there something in the spirit of this run that modulated the most hostile of people and brought on the manners of the delicate and friendly?

Now for the internal individuals. The internal associators are often the elite runners, the ones who keep close tabs on their physical progress, the state of their muscles, the extent of their sweating and thirst. I've often thought it amazing that some of the advice given by the hydrating and nutrition experts is not to drink too much—as in those many articles referred to earlier, particularly those on hyponatremia. And to gauge what's too much, you're advised not to drink more than you sweat. Hello! Are we somehow able to measure our liquid output as well as input, particularly in the heat (so to speak) of battle? Nevertheless, the champions can apparently monitor their hydraulics even as they attend to the condition of their shoes or other equipment. And even on the more modest levels where most runners pin their numbers and their hopes, the attention to those potential blisters or strains or burning sensations must prompt some to adjust to conditions that are occurring and changing rapidly. I would imagine that this does distinguish the individual sport from others, because it's hard to see how in a basketball or football or baseball game, except when the flagrant injury occurs, one can have the luxury, time, or inclination to pay such close attention to incidental impediments or personal bodily quirks.

My running identity, I discovered in training, was that of the fourth type, the internal dissociator. Running for me was such an ordeal, filled with so much strain and pain, particularly at the beginning, that the best way to cope was deliberately to distract myself. Sometimes I'd find myself doing it for most of the run and sometimes just at the most difficult points, like the last stretch or the beginning of hills. I would count anything from the number of days since my last cigar (and count it in many ways—month by month, week by week—since by the end, it had been over two years) to the number of courses I had taught in the last ten years, to the number of different ways you could factor my last running number. I have heard and been told and read that others let their creative selves generate as many such fantasies as will take them, as it were, over hill and dale. One plays back all his elementary school teachers, another visualizes all the women with whom he's been (or, if it doesn't take him to the end of his run, all with whom he has hoped to be). An acquaintance, a bit of a media personality who is often called on to give psychological explanations of crime and criminals, keeps herself going by constructing interviews with famous people she hopes to meet on the air. I have long maintained that doing something with numbers can alleviate extreme suffering. When hostages are in the most deprived and solitary of conditions, how do they preserve their sanity? They scratch the dates on the wall, they keep track of something. Amidst all the confusions and distractions, quantitative and exact solutions offer solace. I may not know what "Get out of here" or "I can't stand you" or "I'm sorry" really means but the square root of 729 is always—despite anybody's moods, despite Derrida and Deconstructionism, despite who's from Mars and who from Venus—27. Is it accident that even in the Bible, following the Exodus and the long haul through the deserts of Leviticus, we have the Book of Numbers? Let's count the sheep and the oxen and the number of generations it's been since Abraham begat Isaac. So yes, all that counting, all that playing with the permutations of my calories or my time per mile or my "METs" (whatever they are) offer a chance to escape the pain. And if we're outdoors, bereft of such proximate distracters, we can invent our own. How many lampposts or trees have I passed, how many days have there been since the last marathon, and how can I figure out when my birthday was in 1985 or even what day of the week I was born on? You don't have to be an *idiot savant* to be so engaged, for mathematicians call people fond of such games "familiar with the numbers;" but I suspect that anyone can do it, after her fashion, because even those without such familiarity can use words and images, like the fantasy movie highlights of their biographies of which some "visualizers" are so fond.

We've come a long way from Heraclitus' effort to distinguish personalities on the basis of which bodily "humour" predominated. But the tendency, as seen in references to "morning" or "night" people or "Type A" and "Type B," still persists. If these are "real," they've yet to be demonstrated, there being even less evidence for any physiological basis. Two other post-Freudian theorists, Adler and Horney, describe types which conceivably manifest themselves readily among runners, although we'd need more empirical support to claim proof. Adler's birth-order typing predicted younger children as being more competitive, having always to catch up with the older.[40] Are you "the older," looking back worried that someone may be gaining on you? Is that what Hendrik Ramaala was doing down the stretch on his way to winning the 2004 New York City Marathon? Horney distinguished those who "move

---

40 Frank Sulloway's 1996 study, described in *Born to Rebel*, is some confirmation of this phenomenon among siblings. F. Sulloway. *Born to Rebel: Birth Order, Family Dynamics, and Creative Lives.* New York: Pantheon; 1996.

toward" others (for example, those who join pace-groups) from those who "move away" (find a little island of space even among 37,000 other runners) from those who "move against" (sense when you're about to pass them and block your movement).[41] Of course, Horney was talking about social interaction, but by now we know that even the metaphor can work literally.

---

41 P. Mullahy. *Oedipus, Myth and Complex*. New York: Grove Press; 1948 (p. 231).

7

Running Amok—
Common Athletic
Pathologies

So much for relatively normal types. But how that list of disorders in the Diagnostic and Statistical Manual does lend itself to the running track. Perhaps every runner is immediately and implicitly aware of all the lunatics that accompany him, but categorizing them runs (follows a path) so much more along the psychological grain. The problem is we've become so attuned to psychologically or technically described illnesses, we become jaded on hearing them.

How casually, for example, "bipolar" is thrown around these days. For a time years ago, there seemed to be a favorite popular star that had to be labeled as one (one month it was Mike Tyson to explain his antics, another Angelina Jolie), and more recently it served as the description given by his significant other to the unfortunate fellow mistaken for a terrorist and gunned down by air marshals. As if that explained why he was announcing he had a bomb. (It might have made more sense if we'd kept the original "manic-depressive" category, since at least we could recognize the "manic" in such behavior.) More recently, an entire session of *House,* another of those sophisticated "medical" television shows (*ER, Grey's Anatomy*) was devoted to analyzing a patient's seeming gibberish and then translating it into a revelation of his inner desires by understanding he was — you guessed it—"bipolar."

Cable-TV news analyst Keith Olbermann, presented with the 2005 White House "holiday" card sent out at Christmastime, asked whether this new sign of political correctness was not in reality a "passive aggressive" message from the President. Okay, I'll play along, he seemed to be saying, if you want to make a civil liberty issue over everything. Olbermann may well have been right, but is everyone so familiar with passive-aggressives? Are we tossing the term around these days as readily and knowingly as the drug companies, hawking the latest antidepressant, remind us of our "chemical imbalance?"

Some characteristics, on or off the playing field, are easy to identify. You defend wearing those outrageous turtle and bunny uniforms so friends will find you in that sea of runners? Sorry, what better example of the exhibitionist can there be? "Here I am, look at what I've got," is the theme song not just of the stripper. Balloons on my head, doughnuts in my ears, Saran Wrap prints from head to toe ... the narcissistic runner is always catching sight of himself in the passing reflectors, be they storefront windows or wading pools, just like the original Narcissus. And they pretend they don't notice your noticing them. For those of us preferring a "natural look," it's a pleasure that women (or men for that matter) runners are usually prevented from wearing too much makeup since they want to avoid the running (flowing, unstopping) mascara or risk looking ridiculous. (Are runners who wear run-proof cosmetics oxymoronic?) And then what about those clothes? Of course some runners prefer their old khaki or gray sweatpants—before the age of Nike Wonders and Super Running Shops, quite acceptable. And of course runners are practical, so the halter top and the bare shoulders and midriff are essential hot-weather attire; but those fuchsias and pinks and chartreuses that tie them all together? And when you catch their glance running in the opposite direction or look back as you pass them, the mascaraless eyelids droop like the female swan's neck in mating season when the male needs to be played with.

"OCD" (obsessive compulsive disorder) has similarly made it to the top of the popular disorder charts, and while that may be because one can't help running into (meeting) it on all walks (or runs) of life, there can be little doubt that it takes a particularly obsessive type to be drawn to this activity of running. The obsessive by definition is governed by an insistence that things must go a certain way, that he must have what he feels he needs, or that he can't vary from his chosen path. My way or the highway, and in this case, my highway. So he catches or avoids every sidewalk crack, lest some catastrophe happen. ("Step on a crack, break your mother's back.")

If he's an obsessive or a compulsive hand-washer, he needs to do it 40 times a day or else cannot eat, cannot go out, cannot live. The idea that numbers play a role here, as we saw they did with "dissociation" types, underscores their importance. Compulsions often involve rituals in much the same manner as religious practices consist of repeating the prayer or Hail Mary or knee bends a certain fixed number of times. Obsessed with the idea of dirt, one overreacts to get rid of it. In fact, I think it fair to say that your typical obsessive-compulsive is possessed by an uncontrollable thought—that is, one that refuses to go away—and in order to try and eliminate it as best he can, he must engage in a compulsive behavior. I am dirty. So I must get clean. But when can you be sure you are clean? As soon as you wash, no matter how thoroughly you wash, you step back into the dirty world and you meet those germs again.

Perhaps it more accurate to say that the obsessive is possessed by an unanswerable question. If I can never be sure I'm clean, the only way to get rid of the thought, "I am dirty," is to act compulsively a fixed number of times. Therefore, I'm clean when I wash 40 times. When am I safe? I've closed all the windows, I've locked my door (or seen to my New York door's six locks), and now I'm ready to go out in the world. But wait a minute. Did I really lock number four? Only one way to tell: I must go back and unlock them all and lock them again. And having locked them again, did I do the second from the bottom? And then did I close all those windows? And what about the gas jets? Were they all turned off? And ... so you can only be sure when you go back a fixed number of times, say five, and unlock those locks three times, *Ave Maria Sancta Spiritus.* So it becomes a dance, the foul shooter on the line, the hitter shaking his head, twisting his hips, banging his cleats with the bat, once this way, once that. Now I know I'm done, I'm ready, I'm best prepared because I've done it 4 or 9 or 613 times.

One of the most common obsessions is the one we have with time, and it is here that we may begin to understand the proximity of this disturbance to running. Obsessives are often extremely punctual because they pay such close attention to time. Or they pay such close attention because they always want to be on time. We want our trains and our watches, of course, to "run on time." Running itself implies time, and being on time. Be he the world record holder or a "back of the packer," what is the first thing the runner checks when he crosses the finish line? His time. And what is the first question asked when you tell someone you've run a marathon? "What was your time?"

The obsession works in the Western world, where salary itself is paid by the clock—even when it's "overtime" or we're working "around the clock," we're obviously paying attention to it—but sometimes, often, it's a bit much. Obsessive patients come exactly on time, never a minute late, and drive the therapist mad (though of course punctuality is a virtue and much preferable to being too early or habitually late). When you've been scheduling patients back-to-back all day, and were looking forward to those 60 seconds to attend to the answering machine or bathroom, you may actually—but please don't tell them —curse the ring of the bell precisely at the 4:00 p.m. starting time of your most obsessive patient. In fact, those who come early to everything tend to be overly anxious about not being on time. So they arrive at the airport four hours early, defending the practice by reminding you of how many checkpoint obstacles it's necessary to hurdle these days—passport check, security check, baggage check, identification check. While those who regularly come late tend to be excessively hostile, symbolically expressing their desire not to be there at all. Think of the places (job, school, mother in law's dinner party) where you're habitually late, and ask whether indeed it's a matter of the trains or the traffic or the terrible weather.

And those who don't show up at all tend to be schizophrenic.

The obsessive runner is careful about most everything, from diet to clothes to time of day. Why? Because indeed, when are you ready? To give your best, to practice as you wish to race, to race your best? How many rehearsals will make you feel adequately prepared? How many activities, from stretching to diet to meditation, can you conceivably find relevant to this practice? Can we not say that there's probably no dimension of life which is not involved in the characteristic ritual practice? And this is all before you step onto the track, before you step out of the house, perhaps before you go to sleep the night before. Am I ready? Once onto the track, we have a host of other characteristics that come into play, from whom you run with to which direction you take to where you set your goal.

The obsessive runner may be indistinguishable from the superstitious one, and there probably is no class of individuals in this world more superstitious than athletes. Yes, Karl Malone couldn't take that foul shot unless he not only did his 11 bounces, but also mumbled some words, perhaps a prayer, under his breath as he prepared to get ready. What are all those unshaven faces doing on the California Angels as they prepare for the playoffs, or those shaven heads on the New York Knicks as they prepare for the basketball playoffs, or those headbands on each of the Detroit Pistons when none of them had any hair? The very idea of wearing the same uniform or socks, or putting them on in the same order or on the same bench, is itself characteristic of the obsessive. Have you seen tennis players forage through that bunch of three or six balls to recapture the one with which they won the last point? Is it really a case of some having more fuzz or less fuzz than the others (these have all come from the same can moments before), thereby being more suited to an Agassi serve? Or is it more likely that one of them is believed to contain the Agassi winning touch engraved somewhere in its Wilson psyche?

So the obsessive runner, wearing for the race the same shorts and shirt and socks that he did during the recent practice run of which he's proud, heads for the course. Did I run three short loops last time in the clockwise direction? Then this time I'll do the same, or exactly the opposite, depending on whether you're a similarity-obsessive or a complementary-obsessive—I've made those terms up, but you get the idea. Was I on the inside of the track or path? Then this time I'll be on the outside. (Track wisdom does suggest not overplaying one side of your shoes over the other, requiring attention to the "crown" of the road, but the obsessive wears his crown a bit heavily.) Did I take a Gu before the start? A power bar? A banana? Four sips of water? Ahh, how the number game, particularly when it comes to food, can rise again. I'll bet there are obsessives who not only count calories in a general way, but in a quite specific one. Ten grams of fat per fig, 4 alpha omega bites of spinach, 125 calories per bagel slice. How many is that? Now I'm ready. Do I run alone or with others? Did I wear that rain jacket thing last time, or did it get in the way? How many times up the hill for speed work? How much of an interval for interval training? How many starts and stops all together? Thinking of how many things there are to count and to alter, to throw together in the mix, it is doubtless of great significance when something works, but for most people the complexity of sorting it out would simply be cause for paying a little less attention rather than more. But the obsessive, like the superstitious or the lottery player or the gambler, believes the secret lies there somewhere, between those numbers that have appeared and have yet to appear, hidden in the birthdays of those you haven't yet tried, and when you run them through (try them in) the machine, you'll either win the jackpot or be doing an 8:29 minute mile instead of 8:30.

The obsessive type is particularly difficult to treat because to a great degree we, the authorities, the architects of precision who run (operate) this business, rely on the structure of the session to lend stability to the world. So without the fixed time, the fixed day, therapy would not be therapy. For many who live in a chaotic world where nothing is quite dependable—who's home, much less when; or who's sleeping where, much less with whom—the therapy session's greatest value is its occurring with regularity. Tuesday at 3:00 p.m., I know where I'm going, like death and taxes, to be changed not by landlord or police or financial problems, but only by *force majeur.* Indeed, on 9/11 I had had five sessions scheduled, and only two, a policeman forced on active duty at 9:30 and another a man from the Bronx who was barred from crossing the Third Ave.

Bridge, didn't make it. Despite the absence of public transportation, despite their having to walk some. How I remember my own shrink during the New York blackout of the 70s talking with pride of one of his patients who arrived on horseback to his office on 56th Street and 2nd Avenue. And during the most recent New York transit strike, when all the buses and subways had stopped, I had only one patient miss, a worker for the transit authority. He was too busy walking the picket lines—or so he said.

So yes, we value our time and place to such an extent that we value those who do so as well and take it as a major sign of pathology should there be constant difficulty with keeping the appointments. And how do you keep it through thick and thin, through terrorist activities and blackouts and transit strikes, through landlord and marital and childcare crises? You have to be a bit obsessive. I must not miss. I must not cancel. I not only will have to pay anyway (a real test of commitment, that), I will lose the trust that has been set up with the therapist as well. I must, like the teacher or student rushing for his classes, like the actor or musician or ticket-holder rushing for the theatre, like the whole Western world, be a bit obsessive. Otherwise things would be a bit too relaxed, perhaps a bit too Zen—which might be fine for the monastery or afternoon siesta, but not for getting the trains to be on time. When the New York Stock Exchange closed for a few days after 9/11, how often did we hear what a remarkable thing it was to get it up and running (operating on schedule) as before, so afraid were we of falling into the abyss had it not?

There's an important parallel here having to do with addiction. We advocate structure, but within structure there must be flexibility. Yes, it's Tuesday at 3:00, but during that hour (or 45 minutes) there's a great degree of freedom. More, we would hope, than practically anywhere. But despite Tuesday at 3:00, the patient is obviously allowed to ask, when there's a sudden meeting or crisis, what about later in the day or week? Not to be able to do that is to be controlled by circumstance, and that is truly to be out of control. Which brings us to addiction.

Some distinction needs to be made between healthy and unhealthy addictions, one that separates the two by some easily definable (well maybe not so easily) characteristics.[42] Like the obsessive, the real addict (that is, the unhealthy one) must—emphasis on "must"—do things a certain way or the anxiety that produces the need is uncontrollable. The bad addict cannot be without it. The alcoholic is defined not by how much he drinks, not by how many jobs or relationships he's lost as a result of his habit, but by whether or not he can leave it. If you must have it, that's a bad addiction. For years, I smoked one cigar, a cigarillo, a night. But I was certainly addicted because I couldn't be without it, even when off in the wilds of the country, walking and stumbling in utter darkness at midnight to find a gas station that happened to have a machine that would dispense some foul-smelling stogie. In fact, not until I started running was I able to give it up, and not without a formidable struggle.

The runners who, obliged to skip a day from their schedule, are depressed or angry, exemplify the bad addiction. Like the true obsessive, they don't control their activity; it controls them. There's nothing wrong with being clean or being safe or ensuring you've done the most to prepare for your turn at bat or a 10K race. There is something wrong with being unable to leave the house without emptying all the drawers in your closet and folding and unfolding the clothes (yes, there are people who do this every morning). There is nothing wrong with circling back on the highway to make sure you haven't struck anything because you heard a noise, but rather with having to do it again and again, generating successive circles that mark,

---

42 A. LeUnes and J. Nation. *Sport Psychology, 3rd Ed.* Pacific Grove, CA: Wadsworth; 2002 (p. 423).

quite literally, how you can't move ahead. This kind of addictive runner compulsively jogs or is obliged to run or is dependent on his exercise, all terms that have been used for a runner whose life is dominated by running and who has given up spouse and children and friends and career and even health in the process. George Bernard Shaw in *Man and Superman* said the true artist must make sacrifices to validate his commitment. How proximate indeed is this kind of art and madness.

At one point in my training, I remember missing two consecutive days for the first time in five months. The first day was Yom Kippur and the second, when I had intended to run, I had an academic "retreat" that ended up taking all day, as they often do. It would have required an immense effort on the second day to get a few miles in. I'd planned to do three, but I could do it the following morning. So I did. I had done my weekly total, aside from the long one I was planning on Sunday (15 miles), but for the moment it did feel like a dangerous business. As if I'd lose the whole preparation, like I was a slacker. It also felt as if something necessary was missing from the day. Running, as difficult as I often found it, helped focus the day, and my mind and body were discovering that. But having more than enough of a reason, I was pleased I'd succeeded (if I could call it that) in not doing it. Discipline can be rewarding, but so can flexibility—something the obsessive knows little of, and that signals a distinctive difference between addictions.

At a poetry reading shortly before his death, I heard Kenneth Koch recite "One Train Hides Another," a piece about a metaphoric series of partners in hiding that was inspired by a sign over a Kenyan railroad track warning passersby (including those with flocks) to be careful. So one sister hides another (always in her shadow), one file hides another (how many items that I was looking for ended up discovered by finding something else in front of them?), one abnormality hides another (it's common for gerontologists to misdiagnosis depression in the elderly as Alzheimer's or dementia), one runner hides another (how many Kenyans do run on each other's shoulders?), and one addiction perhaps hides another. Laurie got over smoking by running. A healthy replacement, but an addiction nonetheless. And how many have gotten over too much eating and even, in my case, too much alcohol? At least, as I've said about exercise for years, it'll get rid of my poisons and (perhaps) get me even.

You can be addicted to something, you can anticipate it with pleasure and look back on it with satisfaction, so long as you're not spending your life admiring your trophies and suspending everything else. Not until they plop you into the nursing home with your photo albums, at least. It's all a matter of balance and moderation and control. It should come as no surprise that the architect of this concept became intrinsic to Greek philosophy (Apollonian harmony vs. Dionysian excess), since where does all this marathon business begin with if not the ancient Greeks? Had Pheidippedes not dropped dead as soon as he reached Athens with the news of the victory over the Persians, I'm sure he would have taken a month off from running and moderately ramped up again.

It should be no surprise that we can find other classic illnesses on the racecourse, enough to arm any stay-at-home-left-in-the-dust spouses with plenty of ammunition to aim at their off-running-again mates. If the paranoid personality is characteristically defined as one who's always looking over his shoulder to see who might be following him, then where else would it show up if not in someone constantly on the move? Of course runners don't look back. Not much, they don't. Take a look at that elite group and how easy it is to see how aware they are not just of who's ahead of them, but who's one yard or one hundred yards behind. To paraphrase Satchel Paige, look back … someone might be gaining on you. These runners, always checking their rearview mirrors, constantly feel that someone is out to get them. Does it provide a sense of control, since they now know whether to turn it on or not (if someone's gaining at mile-17, are you supposed to go faster or let them burn themselves out?), or is it simply indicative of the inability to let themselves be without worrying about what others are doing? Perfect stomping ground for the paranoid.

The most common ailment amongst the general population is depression. The depressive, by definition, is the one who is down, with little appetite for food, for sex, for life, who stays under the covers most of the time. If that sounds familiar, it ought to. Not very many individuals past the age of a year-and-a-half jump up each dawn singing, "Oh, what a beautiful morning." It's common among college students, it's common after you succeed at something (postpartum), it's common after disaster (post-traumatic stress disorder). But in the truly depressed, it stays, and it's not just a feeling of sadness but of hopelessness. What's the sense of getting up or of doing anything?

Actually, there is wisdom in that, since after all, soon we'll all be dead. So what is the sense? But of course to dwell on that future, even to have it in mind too much of the time, explains why, in that extreme form, the depressive contemplates suicide. In fact, exercise in general is so often advocated as therapeutic because no matter how much we complain about going to the gym or getting up or out to do it, it is so life-affirming that it's very hard, at least while doing it, to be depressed. In pain, exhausted, anxious, even angry, yes, those you can be. And if you start doing something ridiculous, like begin running after age 60 to train for a marathon, then isn't it to push that specter of death a little further into the future? While I hardly ever ran before this marathon episode, there was an exception or two, and both had an intrinsic connection to death. Without knowing much of what I was doing, I went out the day after my father died and just started running, and did two miles—which I'd never done before. Let me breathe, my unconscious seemed to be saying in an emphatic way. When my children's mother died prematurely, grief-stricken as they were, they headed for the park to throw snowballs and roll down wintry hills, just to feel, I think, the liveliest parts of nature. Just recently a book came out about a father's taking a cross-country bicycle trip, his wife in the trailer behind, a few years after his son's tragic death in a plane crash, in an effort, if not to get over it, at least to try to come to terms with it.

Martin Seligman, a generation ago, coined the term "learned helplessness" to try and explain the origins of depression.[43] If you put a dog in a cage and shock him for going to one side, he naturally learns to stay in the other. If you then alter the shocking side, he moves first to the non-shocking side but in a while, with continual alternation, he sits down in a corner, unable to move. This, says Seligman, is what's happened to the depressive. He tries one thing, to be a student, fails; tries another, to be a stand-up comic, fails; and eventually ceases to do anything. There are world-class athletes (the predecessor to Lance Armstrong comes to mind) who, following a success, suffer depression and are found in hotel rooms with overdoses of pills. In their case, it's more a matter of failing to see how they will ever live up to their previous billing, and, with no good answer, they surrender to the feeling. Judging from the number of "talking heads" on all the football-preview shows at 11:00 a.m. on Sunday, the majority of whom have been former NFL stars (and not all of whom can be characterized as articulate, clear, knowledgeable spokesmen for their profession, as I've earlier indicated under the "Sport Pundit Phenomenon"), it should not be all that hard for the ex-stars to find something to do. But for many it is. For them it is, in fact, hopeless.

43 W. Miller, R. Rosselini and M. Seligman, "Learned Helplessness and Depression." In: *Psychopathology: Experimental Models*. San Francisco, CA: W.H. Freeman; 1977 (pp. 104–130).

The kind of runner most susceptible to this phenomenon is one who's first had a modest success, not necessarily professional, and then can't do it anymore. Recapturing this success has become for them the only option. For those highly accomplished athletes, it's perhaps natural to grieve for their former selves. But I've also run into (met) many former runners who've stopped because of their knees and, rather than yield, they now walk or get on the other cardio machines or swim or ride bikes. I know of one young mother, a light runner (never more than six miles) who was always out at 5:00 a.m. before her family could miss her, who was so traumatized by an experience with a potential attacker that she never ran again. But she didn't stop moving, exercising, skiing, dancing, and doing yoga to take up the slack. And the current prototype of this kind of recovery is Trisha Meili, the "Central Park Jogger," who was brought to near death by a bunch of thugs and today, over fifteen years later, is not only assisting traumatized victims, but has also run again, including a 4:30 New York Marathon.

In fact, postmarathon depression is common not because most people can't run anymore, but because they actually have given birth to a significant achievement and may feel that there's little that can now top it. So they eventually decide to run another, despite all the immediate oaths not to. I spoke to one runner whose motivation for doing a second appeared different, but actually it was the same sort of thing; she had simply repackaged (or "reframed," as we say in certain therapies) her goal. She'd run her first marathon past anxious parents waiting on the sideline at 80th Street and the park, but because she hadn't been alert enough to tell them which side to be on, they missed her. And so she ran another—just so they'd be able to catch her. Which they did. It was not a new goal, just an unusual one, and it worked. Then, having gotten it in her head that she needed to break four hours (her first two had been 4:01 and 4:07), she ran two more. Never doing it, but always having the goal. What the depressive is doing is surrendering to hopelessness because he can't conceive of a new goal. And that often occurs when he's achieved it. What now?

My most seriously ill patient of late, who actually had to be hospitalized for suicidal ideation (she's fine now), was a young woman who'd fought her way out of the ghetto, had a fine opportunity with a law firm, was beginning college, was having fun meeting men on the Internet, when within a few short months, it all came tumbling down. She'd followed a new boyfriend to another city, relocated, left school, family, and her job, discovered everything—the commute, the school possibilities, the bills—too much, and came back clinically depressed. Why? She felt helpless. She didn't know where to turn as each opportunity was instead a reminder of the failure. Begin school again? Too many unpaid bills. Try dating? Too scared of repeating what had happened before. So she ran back (retreated) to her mother, who was not exactly a representative of progress, having been mired for years in isolation in the ghetto and paying lively attention only to her church. This furthered her depression to such an extent that she couldn't leave her room, and found the only way to break out was to take an overdose of pills and get herself institutionalized. After a day-and-a-half of this kind of "remedial" exposure, she was so anxious to get out of there that she found ways to be a little more productive. Perhaps she needed the close call since, like a reaction to an electric shock, she was jolted into slowly putting her life back together again. While I wouldn't recommend this sequence as a way out of depression, it is perhaps what the addicts mean when they talk of "hitting bottom," and at least for now, it has seemed to work.

This sequence could also be considered an example of what we touched on earlier, of what some sport psychologists believe an essential part of training—the experience of a significant failure in practice so you'll be more familiar with it in reality. If you deliberately shank the golf shot, as Fran Pirozzolo coaches, and it should then happen during the tournament, you won't have to run from it as much. In other words, when we fail in real life, a big cause of our subsequent downslide is that we feel we look so bad to others. That's why tennis, as well as so many other sports, has such "momentum" swings. Make a mistake and you'll make another. Fall on the ice and it'll happen again. I was asked when Eric Heiden did just that in the 1980 Olympics how I thought this would affect his performance, and I predicted it would happen again. Unfortunately, there was no morning line to enable profiting from my omniscience.

It's easy to understand why social psychologists refer to this as "inoculation theory." Take a little of the disease, and you'll be protected against it later. When I tried my first 13-mile practice run in the park and had to start walking at mile 9 because I felt depleted of all energy for some reason (or maybe it was the Gu I'd taken a half mile earlier that might have upset my stomach or equilibrium), I was convinced I was finished for the day. Never having done it before, I didn't like having to lower my goal for fear it would become a habit. But then I caught sight of a water table, there being a triathlon going on somewhere, and managed to start running again and complete the original objective. When subsequently, on a couple of other runs, I also had to stop briefly (say, for a compelling bathroom break or two), I found that although I still didn't like it, I was less worried. In fact, my son advised me that perhaps it was a blessing in disguise; had I simply run every subsequent practice without taking a walk break, should I need one in the Marathon, it might be too devastating.

And he proved prophetic. Two times, first just after the start on the Verrazano and then at the halfway point, I took a bathroom (or a top-of-the-bridge) break, wasted about two minutes in total, but (and I think here's the point) did not regard it as such a severe interruption. Had I started up again, without any history of stopping, I might have felt like quitting entirely as I had during that first practice run. But I'd been inoculated; I quickly got back on the track, particularly after that second stop, and didn't feel I needed to run faster to make up the minute lost. By accepting it, I had minimized it or let it go, and I was then able gradually to catch up. Certainly had I been too frightened to stop, that discomfort of not emptying my bladder might have proven later to be much more severe a handicap. Fail a little and, to put it mildly, you won't think it necessary to end your life because the failure doesn't feel so devastating that it had might as well be the end of the world.

Of course there are other modern approaches to depression, the most evident and trendy being Prozac and Zoloft. What a relief, in a way, to read the latest medical journal reports that the purpose of these serotonin reuptake inhibitors is questionable, since not a single study supports the idea that there's a deficiency of serotonin in medical disorders.[44] In fact, the notion that there is some ideal balance, implied in all those references to "chemical imbalance," is unsupportable.

For years I've been telling students that even if there were such a correlation between mental and chemical states, it wouldn't prove causation, and that the alleged imbalance could very well be a product of the disorder rather than its cause. Don't one's stomach and nervous system and gastrointestinal system start acting up when you're nervous? Would anyone think to say that the sudden pounding of your heart before the interview, or sweating of your palms before you get up on stage, or that urgent need to urinate are causing the anxiety rather than the other way around? One wonders, particularly as these pills are passed around to peers by sophisticated youths acting as psychopharmacologists, how much of

44 S. Begley: "Some Drugs Work to Treat Depression, But It Isn't Clear How." *Wall Street Journal:* Nov. 18, 2005; p. B1.

the benefit sworn to by their users is simply a placebo effect. I've seen at least as many positive results on the couch, of the kind that much of the world, no matter how sophisticated, is apparently still wary.

Particularly athletes. While I can attest immodestly to members of widely disparate groups benefiting from getting their "heads examined," it is not a universally accepted practice of sport participants, despite the lip service we give to the "heart" and the "head." Yes, some sophisticated professional team owners have hired psychologists. At the height of some football scandals—arrests for murder—a few years ago, the New York Giants even administered the Minnesota Multiphasic Personality Inventory (MMPI), a standard personality test, to attempt to weed out potential trouble. When I was asked by a reporter what this could do, I pointed out that the test, which can measure deviation on aggression, for example, hadn't been standardized on a population that is in the business of cracking each other's skulls on the field.[45] So, too, have some athletes in individual sports hired shrinks (recently, as stated elsewhere, the tennis players Martinez, Ginepri and Spadea), but their overall success has not been as influential, apparently, as dopamine and steroids. In an informal survey I took of prospective patients, about twice as many referrals from an "athletic" source (New York Road Runners, for example, where I'm listed along with some car rental companies and chiropractors as a "Members' benefit") didn't show up after making their first appointment, as compared to the rest of the population. And in preparation for the marathon, runners still come with more regularity and listen more intently to the lectures on stretching and nutrition and speed work than they do to the one on psychological factors— one which is always given last, by the way, as if now that they've tried everything else, why not throw in this last prayer?

---

45 J. Angelo. "Shrinking the Giants." *New York Post:* April 11, 1999; pp. 1, 8, 93.

The "bipolar" disorder with which we're now, as indicated earlier, overly familiar, originated as a significant variation on the depressive personality, that being manic-depression. It had first been used to describe people who in some sense were uncontrollable with respect to their own emotions, exhibiting fits of rage and then periods of remorse, for example. This is not quite what the "mood disorder" refers to, but never mind; at least it gave the impression of volatility, which does in fact characterize it.

During the manic phase, there is practically no stopping the person. There has even been recent interest in the topic, exemplified by books on exuberance, by attention to hypomania, by reflections that perhaps this country was founded by maniacs who in turn have genetically passed on these characteristics of euphoria—believing anything possible, taking risks, having great confidence. Some are more cautious, thinking the pathology a dangerous one, as exemplified in the dot com crash, where the nation and the economy actually resembled this personal "crash" that often results from unrealistic expectations.[46] (How many compelling activities am I in the middle of right now—separating laundry, washing dishes, balancing a checkbook, getting dressed for the run, writing about the run, taking notes on the run, finishing the crossword, finishing the expense list, writing the recommendations, opening the mail. And those are just the ones with direct physical evidence on my desk, table, and windows, before I even consider the conversations, new relationships, gift buying, holiday-meal planning and phone calling, in the middle of all of which one could also certainly say I am. Does it all sound a bit much? Not exactly "laid back?" The manic is laid forward.)

Mania—hypo- or regular, high-octane or super, lite or lo-fat— is seductive, contagious and dangerous. By sweeping you

---

46 P. Whybrow. *American Mania: When More Is Not Enough*. New York: W.W. Norton; 2005.

along in her "can't say no" aura, the manic swings fantasy into action as you soar above the mundane (speaking of laundry, dishes and the checkbook). I wonder how many of those biographies I see on dating services are written in a manic state, since everyone's ideal date is flying off to breakfast in PARIS, after bungee jumping into the Guggenheim with a glass of Merlot, followed by walking on a moonlit sandy beach into the roaring fireplace, making a movie together in the Alps, and then winning at the roulette table in Monte Carlo before settling down in Mexico to run a ranch or plant a vegetable garden, all of this sandwiched into a paragraph with LOTS OF CAPITALS, in which they manage to explain that they look equally good in jeans or a black cocktail dress, and are eager to take advantage of all that the city has to offer and have accomplished everything they ever wanted to such an extent that their life is perfect, job extraordinary, family wonderful and friends devoted; but there's just one thing lacking, oh naïve guy out there who's ready to take the bait and jump on the manic bandwagon. I recognize this student immediately in my classes—she's the one, given a choice of topics on which to write her paper, who will effervescently insist that she wants to write all of them and then, as might be expected somewhere along the line, like a dot-com she crashes, and ends up writing none of them. The bipolar description fits, as we wait for the "down" following the "up," which (mania being what it is) can take minutes, months or years.

In a way, the run can be a manic experience. And that may constitute the famous runner's high which, despite my manic tendencies, I am still waiting to experience. There is a feeling of invincibility, in which everything becomes clearer, everything fits. Here, as I'm writing of manic-depressives, I turn on the radio and there's an NPR interview with two experts on the very subject of mania. It's that kind of event, coincidence to be sure, that makes one feel as if somehow he's in charge of the universe or, in Csikszentmihalyi's terms that there's a "flow," that things seem so easy, everything makes cosmic sense.[47] But if a person is continually in this state, chances are that he's delusional because the world, no matter how good and self-actualized you are, doesn't fulfill your desires so readily.

The condition is in essence childlike and perhaps owes its appeal to being so. I remember during the first part of the marathon, when we passed under the first overhanging subway trestle in Brooklyn, runners started shouting to hear the echoes. And this continued every few miles, with each subsequent one. Just like kids. Yes, kids are committed, kids don't think of the "no's"—that's for us to instill in them. And the problem with the constantly manic runner is that the energy can't be kept up, there must be a return to reality or else you'll do something dangerous like run yourself into the ground when you should be resting during training. Perhaps some kind of extreme running (which, if it is called that these days, is not by definition quite the example of moderation or balance) can only be done with this manic investment or personality, but I suspect there are limits to those extremes as well, and that even the "ultramarathoner" had better know those limits or he'll really end up crashing into a real wall. Or having the wall crash onto him.

Let me just briefly mention one further type, to round out some of the classic deviant categories running all about.[48] My

---

47 M. Csikszentmihalyi. *Flow: The Psychology of Optimal Experience.* New York: Harper and Row; 1990 (particularly "The Body in Flow," p. 95).

48 If you haven't kept up with all the "deconstructed" or "reconstructed" more fashionable abnormalities in recent years, you might have fun (on or off the course) with "frontal lobe syndrome" (the defense's explanation for why Dr. Zorro carved his initial in a patient's abdomen), "Perceived Ugliness Syndrome" (the prosecution's explanation for why the witness was afraid of leaving her house), and "Jerusalem Syndrome," particularly lethal around Christmastime and often accompanied by "Messiah complex."

first time back in Central Park, trying to have a modest run after doing the Big One, the question in my head was, "How did I do this?" Four miles seemed as tedious as before. Yes, I had a bit more confidence (at least on the treadmill, as detailed in Chapter One) and felt I wouldn't pass out or have to stop. And I'm wondering if that is why people do it more than once. Because somehow, once is not enough to prove it—once is never enough. Or is it simply that they remember only the good part, the cheering crowd, and not the heavily painful preparation, the intrusion into all aspects of life. I speak of this in Chapter Thirteen, and maybe I have the advantage of knowing I won't do it again, unlike these others who swear they won't when they finish and then go back again. They conveniently forget.

Either that, or they're simply masochists, people who actually enjoy inflicting pain on themselves. The roots of this lie in some guilt a person has about experiencing pleasure, and every runner to whom I've talked who has stopped because of injury with no regret (particularly those who enjoy walking or biking without all that pounding) tells it with a gleeful smile, seemingly recognizing how anyone who keeps doing it must indeed have a bit of the masochist in them. I'm guilty for gaining weight, so I run. I'm guilty that I don't belong to some religion that sweeps me away, so I run. I'm guilty that I can't get more pleasure at home, so I run. The masochist's answer to the pursuit of pleasure is the pursuit of pain, and we can be thankful that for most, it's not the dominant motive. Although I'm not as sure of that as I'd like to be when diagnosing runners.

8

Caught in a Run-Down— Hysterics on One Side, Phobics on the Other

That leaves us only with the hysterics, phobics, schizophrenics (process and reactive, hebephrenic, catatonic, simple, and complex), and those with personality, anxiety, character, and eating disorders. I won't attempt to run (present in serial fashion) all those by you, since although it's quite common to run into (encounter) anorexics and bulimics and schizoids on the subways and streets of New York, these do, usually, manage to stay clear of the running tracks. That is not to say you won't see bingers and purgers and people in one kind of trance or another running with you or against you. But for the most part, it's hard to last very long doing this stuff with those kinds of illnesses. And as for schizophrenics, most easily identified by the characteristic of being delusional (e.g., "hearing voices"), I conclude that all those spokespeople who view running—regular, painful, arduous running—as a source of our most creative thinking or becoming better problem-solvers or "capturing the sounds of the inner world," are indeed hearing and heeding voices, so you be the judge of their pathology.[49]

But hysterics—more often referred to in lay language as "hypochondriacs," those who imagine their ailments—are quite common. And there's nothing like running to promote symptom awareness—from toe to heel, from shin to crown, no muscle or joint or organ is exempt. I mentioned in the first chapter that one of the telling results of my first becoming a runner was an awareness of parts of the body I had successfully managed to ignore for most of my life. But the bright side was that the calves and hamstrings and quads with which I had become too familiar on the tennis courts did not seem often— during or after running—to make their presence known (quite possibly, although you couldn't prove it by my reports, I wasn't usually doing enough of it to so challenge the body), and at least there wasn't runner's elbow or torn rotary cuffs (at least as far as I've heard) to plague one.

But to the hysteric, every twitch is a symptom, every symptom is an incipient disease, and every disease is potentially fatal. And to prevent or cure what they imagine is the worst, they're always at the doctor's or wrapping something or applying some poultice to some spreading wound.

Yes, there's pain—often chronic pain. And yes, there are ways of treating (if not preventing) it, from running with straps or ringlets to taking Tylenol. Many at the medical tent before the marathon are tending to runners with actual difficulties. But there are also people, and most are otherwise healthy souls, who infuse every malady about which they've heard. It is such a common phenomenon that first-year medical students, who hear for the first time of lua lua or schistosomiasis or dengue fever, often start developing the exotic

---

49 A. Burfoot. *The Runner's Guide to the Meaning of Life*, New York: St. Martin's Press; 2000 (p. 64).

symptoms of these diseases. So common is this, in fact, that it's been given the name, "medical students' syndrome."

To complicate further the matter of the "reality" of pain, not everyone is equally sensitive to his or her body. We have different "thresholds" or tolerances or sensibilities, and we're not sufficiently aware of them. If we want not only to recognize what was historically called in American psychology "individual differences," but to understand their origins and see how much change, if any, is possible, we would have to study human development and become familiar with the philosophies of Determinism, Empiricism, Humanism, and Existentialism; the positions of Freud and Jung, with acknowledgments to Aristotle and Montaigne; and the recently burgeoning "health psychology" along the way. Instead, I'll summarize.

Freud placed such a heavy emphasis on childhood because he was determined to be a "Determinist," one who believes that any present event can be traced to a prior cause. All science takes this position (notwithstanding the "uncertainty principle," which applies more to the inadequacy of our measuring instruments than it does to a world of random events or uncertainty), for how else does an engineer or chemist or doctor try to account for the damage? The earache (or bridge collapse or explosion) didn't just happen, but had to result from some prior event or series of events. We may differ in how far into the past we go—Aristotle himself distinguished proximate from distal causes—or in whether we attribute the cause to the bacteria in the ear or to my having been in a hurry last week (or all my life) and leaving the house without an umbrella. We may be at a loss to discover the cause, but there is no scientific doubt that there is one.

Freud extended this concept to psychological events. The infamous "Freudian slip" is as good an example as any that there is meaning to the most incidental of activities, that nothing we do is uncaused. And our personalities are formed early, in the first five years of life, for the most part. It was Jung's hypothesizing of the extrovert/introvert dimension, discussed in Chapter Six, that later led to research on newborns and showed differences in sensitivity to the environment, some nervous systems being more "labile" than others. This supports the argument explaining differences as largely genetic.

The problem with the deterministic world view is not only that we don't like it because it makes us robotic prisoners, but it isn't consistent with our most emphatic experience in being human, which is that we're free. I may get into trouble, but I can do what I like. So Humanists enter the stage to insist it's up to us to break the chains of the past, that everything takes place in the present. They emphasize "will" and "becoming" and "actualizing".[50,51,52] Their relatives, the Existentialists, even as they write about there being "no exit" from the human condition, proclaim their objection to the deterministic stranglehold on our freedom by asking, "The way out is through the door; why is it so few will take it?"[53] But of course the runners, particularly those who've heard from the beginning that the hardest step is the one taking you out the door, do.

I am tempted to say that whether it is at all easy to do this depends on how discomfort and illness and pain have been treated in your history. If you did stay home every time you had a sniffle—perhaps because in childhood it was the only way you could get those busy parents to pay attention to you—then chances are you will listen very closely to what your body tells you and behave cautiously (as did Justine Henin-

---

50 R. May. *Love and Will.* New York: W.W. Norton; 1969.

51 C. Rogers. *On Becoming a Person: A Therapist's View of Psychotherapy.* New York: Houghton–Mifflin; 1961.

52 A. Maslow. *Toward a Psychology of Being.* New York: Van Nostrand Reinhold; 1968.

53 J. Sartre. *No Exit + Three Other Plays.* New York: Vintage; 1973.

Hardenne, to the chagrin of many, when "retiring" in the 2006 Australian Open final because of an upset stomach). If you grinned and bore it, or if you didn't need dramatics to gain your parents' attention, then your tolerance for that strained, sprained, inflamed muscle may be just that much greater. Some medical authorities suggest that, up to a point, it's even better to exercise hurt than to rest. I'm not arguing which is preferable, but simply noting that you can justify both positions in sport as you can in life; and perhaps being at different ends of this spectrum accounts for some disputes among couples, one thinking he doesn't take care of himself enough and the other thinking she's too self-indulgent.

And do we not hear from the running pundits contradictory advice on this very subject? On the one hand, you have to push yourself, the body is always jarred at the beginning of a run, you have to be hardy and survive the temptation to quit because of rain or pain. On the other hand, you should never run if your body doesn't feel right.

So how do we know? I suggest you find out where you are on the thin-skinned, thick-skinned dimension ("no judgments," as the Sports Club says) and adjust accordingly. Let my kids, as usual, be the prime examples. It occurs to me that I have an Odd Couple of children, no matter how similar their values or current interests. They illustrate how basic is this difference in sensibilities, one that seems quite independent of the kinds of treatment or experience mentioned above. Matthew, in his high chair, loved foods mushed together and didn't shy away from mustard on his hot dog (or face, or shirt) from the start. To this day, 30-odd years later, his desk (and mine, too, I should add) has the same characteristics of a warzone that his tray and the floor beneath resembled after his six-month-old self's meals. As "expressive" as was Matthew's gastronomical environment, so was Benjamin's equally fastidious. He would loudly complain if a strand of spinach so much as kissed a kernel of corn or brushed a mound of mashed potato, as if he were a rabbi watching a kid seethed in its mother's milk. But I came to see that it wasn't just obsessiveness or a primitive fear of being poisoned (we'll come to the phobias, shortly) or what we shrinks like to call "oppositional tendencies" renowned in the (terrible) two-year-old. He simply could tell, like the princess with the pea under her mattress, if there were a touch of olive or pickle or (heaven forbid!) mustard in the most integrated, well-stirred, well-cooked dish. Try taking advantage of the "all-the-toppings-you-want" deal at the local pizzeria? "Plain cheese, please." Maybe, if feeling particularly adventurous, "extra cheese." As for smell, were he within a quarter-mile of a cigarette (much less a cigar), he would start running (putting one foot rapidly in front of the other) in the opposite direction. Maybe that's where it started.

If it's only a matter of taste, "thin-skinned" articulates differences better and allows you to distinguish Bordeaux *soixante-deux* from *quatre-vingt*. But it's also less adventurous. If you stay away from pepperoni and anchovies, how welcoming will you be of braised eel with leeks and polenta in béchamel sauce at the king's reception? The sensibility, however, radiates to the tactile as well. For years, mustard-hating son couldn't walk, much less romp, around if a coagulated part of his sock hadn't been straightened out before being immersed in his sneaker, or if the knot on his scarf was rubbing his neck ever so slightly. But mustard-friendly son wouldn't notice if he'd lost a glove until, literally, the snow had so coagulated on his fingers that he had to wonder why the football kept slipping out of his hand. Do not these differences say something about the ability to withstand pain? Is it likely that it's all learned? Can it all simply be a matter of will?

As a final note of confusion, here's a small contribution from the growing field of health psychology. We're learning more these days about how much control we have over ourselves, even with respect to physical problems and disease. The role of psychological factors in illness is receiving more attention. Stress is a factor, even in causing dental problems. Depressed people get more heart attacks, and survive less often once they have one. Even prayer seems to have a beneficial effect on remission possibilities. Early bodily differences are real and later experiences influential (paranoids have real enemies and hysterics have real pains), but they're not prescriptive. Look at Trisha Meili.

If the question of "hysteria" ultimately depends on a matter of sensibilities, it certainly doesn't seem true of other abnormalities. Did I say I'd exhausted all of them? The odd thing is that once you open up the list of diagnostic categories, they all start sounding so familiar. Consider what's sometimes thought of as the most restricted ones, the phobias, whereby individuals become extremely anxious when exposed to quite specific stimuli, be they objects or situations. Phobics can live a relatively normal life, so long as they're not brought into contact with what they fear on more than a sporadic or casual basis. The more serious pathologies—OCD, paranoia or bipolarity—radiate throughout the person's thinking, feeling, and behavior. Or at least, a lot of it. The obsessive is not just a "neat-freak" about his desk. He's compulsive about time or safety or supermarket shopping. To be sure, not everyone performs rituals over everything. But the disorder is debilitating because it takes over one's life. It's hard to dress for success if you're spending all your time emptying your dresser drawers and refolding your clothes. If you are obsessed with making money (probably because somewhere along the way you not only learned how this concern might benefit you, but were made to feel extremely anxious over the specter of being poor), you'll probably be forever worried about keeping it. To this day, one of my patients feels a panic whenever he reaches in his pocket to get his wallet (which he knows is there, for he felt it a minute ago), an outgrowth of his parents' overly strong attachment to money when he was a child. It has become an end in itself and seriously hampers his ability ever to enjoy it.

By contrast, if he is afraid of spiders, the arachnophobic can usually succeed in avoiding them (except in the movie version). Even where the source of the fear is a situation rather than an object (claustrophobia, acrophobia), the victim is not without ways of coping. One relative of mine, terrified of heights, could go up in elevators, but not alone. So it was something of a nuisance or embarrassment (waiting in the lobby for someone to come along and having to withstand the stares of descending passengers should he be there for an extra long time), but he managed to live an otherwise productive life. And people who can't stand being in a closed-off space, despite our insulated world of insulated cubicles, usually find a window or door to be near or else simply avoid that kind of environment.

Despite being described by many runners as "boring," treadmill running may simply not work for some because it induces a kind of claustrophobia, situated as the machines usually are in a narrow, limited, closed-in environment rather than the great outdoors with potentially unlimited vistas. There could be other phobias at work here as well, as you're typically in rather close proximity to strangers. Not quite as bad as a New York subway in rush hour, when you can literally sniff each other's odors, but close enough to get more than a whiff. The xenophobic needs only that to start feeling anxious. And when you combine these conditions, as at the start of the New York Marathon atop the Verrazano Bridge, you have the potential not just for xenophobia and agoraphobia (fear of the outside, although this might be a bit prohibitive for someone about to do 26 more miles), but also for acrophobia (fear of heights, made a bit more salient by the pounding of 75,000 feet causing this longest bridge in North America to shake) and hydrophobia (fear of water), to say nothing of "transhydrophobia" (crossing water)—which we may be thankful has been deleted from medical dictionaries along with 400 other phobias popular at the beginning of the last century, when doctors were beginning to think all mental disturbance was phobic—all rolled into those first two miles. At those medical tents before the start of the race, you do see many individuals who are seeking not just Vaseline, bandages, or massages, but some solace for their anxiety, the source of which is often out of their awareness.

Phobias appear to be the disturbances most treatable by therapy, but chances are that even the most experienced practitioner is not going to be able to accomplish that in the hour or two before a marathon. Problems like those described above have been addressed successfully by behavioral approaches, which create a learning environment in which the subject is taught to relax while being gradually confronted with the object of his fear. Don't throw the arachnophobic into a basement overrun with giant killer spiders from South America (if you do remember the movie), but first show him a picture of a spider, have him relax (play his favorite music), and then, perhaps, introduce a live but itsy-bitsy spider, and so on up what's called a hierarchical ladder that rises to the true object of his fears. Not a "sink and swim" approach, but "systematic desensitization." If he learned (as behavior therapists argue, because everything to them is learned) his phobic behavior (say, by getting stuck in an elevator once and experiencing a real panic), then it can be unlearned.

But again, this is not an approach that has time to work like meditation or stretching before a race. Even hydrating and carbo-loading take some time to be effective. Therefore, what's critical is to identify these kinds of problems early enough for treatment. People are known to be afraid of abstract objects as well—like numbers—and learning a little system beforehand (as New Yorkers well know, or knew before the tax went up another percent, double the tax to determine the tip) can prevent your either going to extremes to avert anxiety (avoiding restaurants or cabs) or else becoming overly generous so as not to feel guilty about leaving too little.

In fact, the last behavior is what is referred to, for obvious reasons, as "counterphobic" behavior. So determined are we not to let our phobic anxieties limit us that we adopt the opposite behavior. In the literature on defense mechanisms, discussed in the next chapter, this is also known as a "reaction-formation," whereby we're forming a reaction against the feeling we have by adopting a behavior opposite to that dictated by the feeling. Afraid of climbing the mountain, we're the first in our group to rush on ahead. Ashamed of being labeled stingy, we donate overgenerously. Some adults still lead their lives in counterphobic reaction against their parents. One patient I treated couldn't abide being careful with money, since her parents had been. So she not only indulged herself, but got furious if her mate wouldn't splurge on a $15 glass of wine or if he ever let money affect his decisions. Extremely anxious about sexual talk or scenes because we're so attracted to them and afraid to admit it, we make censorship our career, making sure that all is safe for the general public by watching every movie that might have explicit or implicit sexual content. That, needless to say, doesn't leave many out.

I'm suggesting that being overly zealous about anything—and does exercise come to mind as a prime example?—is characteristic of one who is afraid of what will happen if he stops or delays or takes a vacation. So terrified is he of "letting himself go" that he is vigilant to a fault, and in the case of runners, always "on the go." While "rest days" now seem to be recommended during even the most rigorous of training schedules (and certainly for longer periods following long races), how many marathoners did I see up and down those Central Park hills within days of having completed the marathon?

I've noted also that professional tennis players have injected "periodization" into their playing schedules, taking time off and not playing every tournament, even though it may hurt their ranking. Natalie Dechy, one of France's top players, said in 2005 that she wouldn't play more than three tournaments in a row and, particularly after the major tournaments, she'd rest for three days. The problem with running advice, as we've indicated elsewhere, is that there are implicit contradictions, for even as we're told to allow for recovery and older runners especially are told not to do it every day or even every other day, we're also provided five- or six-day-a-week schedules and anecdotes about amazons who've run every day for 100 years. When I first immersed myself in training for my first race, I was limping thereafter for a couple of months, so clearly some "underzealousness" is more advisable. On the other hand, I hadn't noticed Ms. Dechy in the 2006 tournaments, so one wonders whether "periodization" is the first step toward taking up golf.

One further note on therapeutic approaches. If one can't do any real behavior therapy in the modest time before a race, then surely there's even more difficulty attempting to be a "depth" therapist. When I suggested during a lecture on "visualization" that, of course, as with any other activity or problem, one needed to work out all sorts of issues in running (like why one felt compelled to run alone, or to stop and walk before the finish line, or to run at all) if one were interested in knowing as much about himself as possible, there seemed to be a general groan from the audience; not from suspicion about this possibility, but rather from knowing that you can't really expect to resolve all your Oedipal issues with three weeks left before the marathon, can you? "Well, you're beginning to taper, aren't you," I was tempted to say. What better way to spend your time? It is important to realize, if in fact one wants to know about therapy for all kinds of problems, that even though something may seem to work, it may only be for a limited time (and certainly the HMO insurance overseers that are now the payers for a majority of therapeutic sessions try to make treatment shorter and cheaper). The psychoanalysts, even when confronted with what appear to be some success stories, have always been of the mind that all this approach does is address symptoms, not the disease. You may get rid of a smoking problem through desensitization and reward; but worthwhile as that may be, it will simply be replaced by another symptom if you haven't treated the cause. Indeed, this is called "symptom substitution." So the "cured" smoker often overeats, precisely what the analyst predicts, since the real problem is not the smoking but the great attachment to oral pleasure. It's as if you cured the patient by getting rid of his high temperature and failed to eliminate the virus or bacteria or wound that was responsible for it.

So, yes, we can get people to cross that (Verrazano) bridge when they come to it by introducing relaxing experiences, but how much better if we can get them to cross it before they come to it, by understanding themselves better and why they do what they do. And if you've managed to escape serious pathological categorization so far, rest assured you'll find yourself among the "normal" users of the mechanisms by which we try not to know ourselves.

9

Run for Cover—
Defense Mechanisms

Yes, we've become almost too familiar with the most primitive defense; and no, "denial" is not a river in Egypt. Not wanting to accept bad news, we simply discount it. The doctor mixed up the X-rays. It couldn't be me. She couldn't have, she's my best friend. Denial of the bad medical news is quite common. Denial of death, in fact, is a commonplace of our culture. We do this by talking of the deceased as if they're somewhere, looking down at us, guiding us. Is that a distortion? Defense mechanisms do protect us but by distorting the truth, by altering reality. In many instances, however, they also enable us to cope.

The stark reality of death (or illness, or infidelity) can prove debilitating. When James Blake referred to his father as guiding him through some of his magnificent moments on the tennis court, it probably gave him an incentive to continue and play superbly.[54] As was reported so frequently, Blake had

---

54 In the 2005 U.S. Open he defeated second-seeded Nadal—the biggest winner of the year other than Federer, and conqueror of Federer in the French Open. Blake then went on to lose in the fifth set to Agassi in the quarter-finals, in what will probably be a highlight film forever.

been through a series of traumas that year—not just the death of his father, but a serious case of shingles which almost left half of his face paralyzed. Yet he came back to play his best tennis ever.

So do we need to dress up the corpse as if he were still living? Do we need to refer to him by every euphemism possible? On a "journey," on the "other side," having a "homecoming," "passed on," "passed away," or just "passed?" I had a close relative who dreamed each night for 20 years that her father was still alive and returning to talk to her. He had died prematurely and his illness had been hidden from her since, she being only twelve at the time, it was felt she couldn't "handle it." What couldn't be handled was the sorrow that all were feeling and the uncertainty about how to share that with a young girl. In the long run, over an extended period of time, she would have handled the truth much better than believing that her father was just missing and about to return, as her dreams indicate.

We deny our sexuality; we deny that of those close to us. It's a cliché that we can't imagine our parents having sex. If we suspect our spouse of being unfaithful, we may vigorously pursue the truth, but it can cut both ways. We may not wish to prolong a relationship that should have already ended, but we also wish to keep something intact, the elimination of which might cause even worse pain. Should someone inform the mother of eight children, who has no means of livelihood for herself, that her husband is having an affair, or is she indeed better off not knowing, even when she knows, even when she denies?

It's probably better to face, and not to deny, injury. If you don't like the doctor's report, you're free to get another one, but if you search the world hunting for one that's favorable, you're likely to be ignoring a condition from which you can't escape. And yet, if the athlete faces all that's true about him, that he'll never be as good as he once was, he might lose the incentive to get out there at all, and become, as was discussed earlier, severely depressed. Which can have even more severe consequences. If, however, your denial is part of your public relations campaign, and if it involves egregious distortions (like claiming you're really running six-minute miles when you're doing eight, and cutting 25 percent off your real age), there is likely to be a greater cost at the end.

We rationalize, we project, we identify, we displace, we sublimate. We engage in such behaviors to reduce the likelihood of attack from any set of directions, even if we do so unconsciously. A prime example of how and why we rationalize can be found in the manner in which we face rejection. Say that I'm a guy trying out for a school team; I work hard toward my goal, have been gearing for it all year long, and end up failing by not making the cut. Am I then "no good?" Or, at least, not good enough? How much more convenient to say that it's better this way, that I'd have to practice so often, so hard, that I wouldn't be able to do anything else (like study). Or that the coach had it in for me. Or that I really didn't want it anyway. Now substitute "marathon running" for "making the team." No, it's not easy when you can't do it, when you haven't practiced enough, when you couldn't complete the training runs or the long runs, to be able to say that you'll wait till next year and ignore the time and energy put in and the number of people informed of your objective. But you find a way. This is not the right time for me. I haven't been able to practice enough. I'd probably hurt myself. That all of these things could be true doesn't diminish their being rationalizations. They're good reasons, not the real reason. The real reason is that you might fail.

I became aware of my own favorite running rationalizations right after the marathon. It's all right now (finally!) not to run. Which indeed it was, and certainly high on the experts' recommendation list, along with quickly finding something else to do for at least a week or two. And then, after six days, when I figured that if I stopped entirely I'd never go back, I ran three miles down the same East Drive by the Park where I had but three miles to go on November 6th, telling myself it's all right to go slow. Which of course it was. After all, my body needs to rest. I've just (almost just) done 26.2.

And then it occurred to me that I had used the same reasoning when I hadn't run in awhile, when exactly the opposite was true. Take it easy. Your body's not used to it. After all, doesn't everyone say that? Break it in gradually. Don't ramp up too much. That's how you get injured.

So how different can running be from life? Did I find all kinds of reasons not to do something because they were valid, or simply because I wanted to find reasons not to do something? I wanted to take it easy. I'd been working hard. I deserved to. I was entitled. I want to take it easy because I'm not used to it. I don't have to be the star. It's new to me.

New or old, familiar or unfamiliar, we find good reasons. Run less, taper, take more days off as you approach marathon day. But still run 30 miles or 60 percent of your highest mileage per week! (That one always got me. Was everyone running 50 a week or ten a day?) And though they're not the true reasons, they work. That's what good excuses do. They're convincing. And they're more likely to operate this way when the advice or lessons are contradictory. That way we can cite authority, no matter what we do. Remember that Shakespearean metaphor, "the Devil can cite scripture for his purpose"?

I don't have to do it, or do it fast, because I didn't get enough sleep, have a few aches, am a bit dehydrated, just played tennis, will soon be playing tennis, (and my favorite) don't have the time because I have to write (about running). And whenever I leave it for later in the day, the temptation to rationalize gets even greater. It seemed that for each hour that went by, there was twice the chance I'd find a good reason not to. It's what I've termed the "rationalization-graded equation." Perhaps you're familiar with "age-graded times," an obscure formula (and rarely published, in my experience) for equating peoples' running times, regardless of how many decades they've been around? Take your actual time and subtract the number of years you're over age 32 multiplied by the ratio of the distance of the race to 13 (it knocked over an hour, I'm happy to say, off my marathon time). Got it? Never mind. Excuses for not running on a given day equals two times the number of hours after 8:00 a.m. you haven't yet run. That's easy.

We could also "project." Literally, throw forward. The way a movie projector throws an image onto a screen and a project is something thrown forward in time (i.e., not done overnight) and a projectile is a missile thrown into the air. So we throw our own characteristics onto another, thereby thinking we're rid of them. Afraid to climb that mountain, we can act counter-phobically, as described in the last chapter; or we can project, walk over to our fellow adventurers and, noticing that they look scared, assure them they've got nothing about which to worry.

We remember everyone who's ever shortchanged us. We can count how many times we picked up the check, had to bring the tennis balls, gave gifts that were never reciprocated. Who else but one keeping such close track, to whom it means so much, would be able to recount all those instances? Why do I get annoyed at so many "helpful," supportive individuals who told me before the big race that it was okay to fail? "Yes, it's a fine objective," said one. "But you know, I remember all those people who put so much stock into doing natural child-birth, and then when it came down to it, they couldn't do it. What if that happens to you?" Or, "well it's okay to walk also, you know, if you can't make it all the way." "Hey, you've done a half (or 16, or 20), you can just walk the last 13 (or 10 or 6)." Of course, I knew all that. I'd had it somewhere in the back of my mind, but I certainly didn't want to be too conscious of the possibility. And what, really, were they doing? Isn't it a projection of sorts, a way of coping with their own disappointments and seeking the reassurance that another's failure would make things more tolerable? Not exactly *Schadenfreude,* but close.

There's another kind of projection, less common and perhaps more interesting. For the most part, it's our negative characteristics, naturally enough, that we project—our stinginess, cowardice, failure, hostility ("What are you looking at?" wonders the paranoid, projecting his attention to everyone onto them). But we can also do so with the positive. It's a subtle or not-so-subtle recognition that not everyone in this world is so happy to see we've done well. Get great grades? Then you walk around congratulating those who do moderately well because you know you'll be standing out too much if you're standing alone. Can't help but be very attractive? Then you notice how "good" she's looking. "Did you do your hair differently; that looks really great on you!"

So while it's nice to hear that our form or our time or our running accomplishment is "really good," it begins to wear thin when you hear it too often from the same source, one you know is that much better. Call it patronizing or call it projection. I'll believe it much more when the same cheerleader has earlier told me the opposite, even euphemistically, that I was really—as the commentators say when the quarterback or foul shooter or server has missed a dozen passes, shots or serves in a row—"struggling."

Identification has been described as one of the healthier forms of defense—remembering that they're all methods of coping, hence a form of adjustment, hence potentially healthy—in that we need to engage in at least a bit of it to become what we wish. Minorities suffer, it's sometimes felt, not so much from sociological or economic deprivation as they do from a lack of "role models." Certainly an athletic star invites many a child to form identification. And not just kids. Look at those football and hockey jerseys (Jeter, Jordan, Gretzky) worn to games by fans, who feel for a couple of hours that it is they who are actually out on the rink or playing field.

Runners may be slightly more sophisticated than that. We don't see Ramaala or Prefontaine logos above the numbers on the race t-shirts—although, in commemoration of New York Marathon founder Fred Lebow or nine-time winner Grete Waitz, there are wrist bands to wear. This is not so much identification as it is honoring a hero or a family member (in the sense of running or swimming or biking to raise funds for and awareness of various illnesses; both Lebow and Waitz are cancer victims, with Waitz's battle ongoing). But there is a more important form of identification that surrounds the activity, and that is, put simply, the identification of oneself as a runner. This may not seem like an identification with another, but it is the outgrowth of that and has important consequences.

The first form of identification that originates in childhood is with the parent. It is a way of coping with our smallness and lack of power. Typically we identify with the same-sexed parent, although there are variations. The daughter dresses like mother, puts on her mother's makeup, plays with dolls in a "motherly" way. (Not to be "sexist" about it—even though gender clearly plays an important role in the identification—for little boys, if their fathers have played a nurturing parental role, can act similarly.) When that parent is not around, or for some reason not a good "role model," we can find other family members, even an older sibling, or look outside to the media, to our culture, to our immediate environment. How many little Pelés have there been in the Brazilian soccer schoolyards over the last two generations?[55]

---

55 No comment on the dilemma French kids must be facing, now that Zidane's head-butt is more renowned than his penalty kick.

Eventually the automatic identification can become more conscious as one thinks, "Gee, how would daddy react in a situation like this?" If the identification is strong, you actually integrate the idealized figure's characteristics into your personality. These, obviously, can be good or bad, depending on the range of such characteristics that are displayed. That daddy is a bon vivant, a social animal, does not necessarily mean you should want to adopt his drinking habits, particularly if excessive, but you do. And that is often how people become athletically minded; they take on the role of that important figure. Not by accident do a host of professional athletes (there are currently four NFL quarterbacks—Griese, McMahon, two Mannings—who are sons of former NFL quarterbacks, and by the 2006 All-Star Game there were 14 examples of fathers and sons who had both played in these games) follow literally in the footsteps of their heroes. And what could be simpler and more direct than following in the footsteps of someone who runs?

But since running, however long its literal history, is a relatively new sport, judging at least by its general popularity, the runner's identification as such depends more on his own performance. I can attest to that. All my life, running, being the farthest thing from an activity in which I participated, was hardly something with which I could identify. I'm reminded of what I said earlier was my son's reaction when I completed that marathon: "Well now, dad, you can call yourself a runner." And what really does that mean?

I've done some research on the subject. What it means is that even if I never run again, something can't be changed. I might stop, but chances are I'll go back, even if just for a visit.

Everyone stops everything. No one pursues relentlessly, except the truly obsessive or exceptionally single-minded, any goal without interruption. But the important question would seem to be whether he or she goes back. The question is not why people give up dieting, as everyone does, but whether you consider yourself a thin or healthy person. Don't go back, and you don't have that identification. You want to cure or, at least, minimize the school dropout problem? Then focus your energies not on the sociological or economic conditions which affect so many, particularly minorities, but on the question of student identity. I've instituted a policy of labeling students' t-shirts with numbers like runners, so even if they have to stop, they'll see themselves as students. Make a big fuss. Have a ceremony. What's the purpose of the elaborate reception to celebrate a marriage? Or of having an unforgettably exotic honeymoon? R.D. Laing wrote of it years ago.[56] To establish, to drill in an identity. There is no one who doesn't wake up the next morning wondering, "What have I done?" (Or the previous morning, wondering, "What am I about to do?") What does it mean to be a wife, a husband? I don't feel married. I don't want to feel married. So to diminish the doubts, to stamp in the identity, there's all that hoopla. Take a look at the pictures. You're a bride. You want to run away? Sorry, there's all that flatware to return.

In short, without the identification that usually starts with what we're accustomed to calling a "role model," we don't really know who we are. There are periods when we may lose sight of it, when we may try on different selves, but this is all potentially healthy because it means we're choosing instead of just being thrust into it.[57] We may also lose it when we lose a life partner, through death or divorce, for example—who am I if not X's husband, if not the essential part of that couple?—and this is a cause for identification with the deceased, as many begin to take on characteristics of the loved one in an

---

56 R. Laing. *Politics of the Family.* New York: Pantheon; 1971 (p. 69).

57 Erik Erikson refers to this as the crisis occurring in late adolescence or early adulthood between identity and identity diffusion, which was originally referred to as "role confusion."

unconscious effort to keep him or her alive. This can work, but it's also potentially dangerous if the incorporated charac- teristics are ego-alien, if they don't fit, if we're stretching our- selves to become someone we're not. So the question about any identity, including that of runners, is whether or not, even though we've started because of others and continue with a group of others, we've really come into it ourselves; whether, in the popular vernacular, we "own it." If not, no amount of proper running gear will cover it up.

There are those, Freud included, who believe that most of modern civilization reflects a sublimation of our primitive drives and instincts. We push something down (sub=under; lim=threshold) and cover it with something else. We make art, we make war, we make deals as a substitution for making love, which we want to do all the time, or at least a lot of the time, but can't for various reasons. So we channel the sexual drive into an area that's creative rather than procreative. And the aggressive drive into a friendly competition (or even a "cut- throat" one) that doesn't destroy the opposition. (Except of course for those psychopaths who don't or can't, and end up sooner or later getting locked up or living the life—or suicidal death—of the terrorist). The beasts of the field follow their instincts; they do not sublimate. And they do not make histo- ry. Or write books. Or run just for fun.

All of sport is a prime example of sublimation. We pound, kick, drive the ball toward the bleachers, goal line, or cup so as not to pound or kick our real opponent. Or if you want to take a slightly more risqué approach to those two basic instinc- tual drives, it's not aggression that's being substituted for, but sexuality as well. Before we even talk about "defending the red zone" or the "crease" against penetration. In some cases— boxing seems to be the best example—the sublimatee isn't so distant from the sublimator, but at least it's with gloves on and there seem to be certain rules.

Is running a substitution for something else? As with all play, or things we don't have to do but like to do, yes. The intellectual play, be it chess or poker, the play that offers a big jackpot and is largely based on luck, be it roulette or the lottery, are basically substitutions for work. We want to outsmart our opponent at the table where the stakes (for most of us) are not life and death. We want to hit the winning number and break the bank so we don't have to work for it or rob it. Whereas we once ran because we had to, to escape our predators or forage for survival, our running apparatus is still there when it's no longer a necessity (perhaps in a few evolutionary stages our legs will be replaced by accelerator and brake pedals, but for the present our mobility is not automobility, no matter how much of a "self-starter" our résumé says we are). Research that I touched on in earlier chapters suggested a number of characteristics that we developed during our evolution prove highly suitable to running. Everything from heavy buttocks (which stabilize the trunk; apes don't have them and they can't run so well) to short toes to the nuchal ligament, which keeps our head steady, facilitates this. It may be that all this began some two million years ago when we moved from forest areas to the plains and thereby had less of a need to climb and more to move quickly—that ligament doesn't appear to be present in our ancestors before two million years ago—but there it is.

So we used to be able to run because we had to, and now, limited as we are to running to the bank or post office before it closes, we choose to run. Because we don't have to. Because it's play. Tell it to the elite runners who run the equivalent of a few marathons a week. Okay, maybe not for them—after all, $160,000 (the women's' first prize in the 2005 New York Marathon) for a couple of hours may just provide an incentive for which to work—but it wasn't exactly a strong motivator for the other 37,000. In the same way that the car, once a luxury, is for most Americans now a necessity (don't get me started again on cell phones), running, once a necessity, is now a luxury. The defense mechanisms rest.

10

The Motor's Always Running— Motivation

Everyone knows what it is—sports pundits nattering on about its necessity in athletes, crime investigators assuring us of the necessity of discovering it in alleged perpetrators, and educators bemoaning its lack in students these days. But while motivation once occupied an important place in psychology— particularly in the areas of personality and testing, although it was particularly influential as it spawned much research in "achievement motivation"—it has tended of late to take a back seat in the academy, a victim, along with psychoanalysis, of more behavioral and cognitive approaches. This constitutes, to my mind, sufficient reason for bringing it back to the front.

Freud's earliest work with dreams (they're to be understood as "wish fulfillments") and errors ("slips" aren't slips), comprising the bulk of the *Introductory Lectures in Psychoanalysis,* affirm his belief that we are what we want .[58] If you want to understand a person, you don't simply describe his behavior as a product of learning or reinforcement, as do the Behaviorists (most notably, B. F. Skinner). Such views essentially regard man as a passive organism, much like a robot that simply "outputs" what it inputs. You want to know why a person runs? According to the Behaviorists, it is because early on he got rewarded for running, and so it becomes a habit. Not very complicated. Conditioning, like Pavlov's dog. Well, not exactly, since Pavlov's experiment demonstrated that classical conditioning and reinforcement involves a different kind, but close enough. In fact, Governor Mike Huckabee implies this system of analysis when he tells us to be mindful of the reward system if we want to keep up a certain habit, as he did when he lost 100 pounds and then ran his first marathon.[59]

A person comes late or runs or becomes a dentist because he got reinforced for that behavior he now manifests. Later theorists modified it a bit and allowed that imitation or "modeling" could also explain why one would be prone to pick up characteristics of those around him, most notably his parents (dentists don't usually practice dentistry at age five, so it's hard to get reinforced for it), but the model was still essentially the same. People became reinforced for picking up what others demonstrate or value.

But that approach, according to others, is not only simple-minded, it also leaves out the essential part of what makes us human. So Abraham Maslow and Carl Rogers heralded the arrival of the so-called Humanists, those devoted to restoring

---

58 S. Freud (J. Strachey, trans.). *Introductory Lectures on Psychoanalysis*. New York: W.W. Norton; 1966. Lectures 2–4 are on "parapraxes" and 5–15 on dreams.

59 M. Huckabee. *Quit Digging Your Grave with a Knife and Fork: A 12-Step Program to End Bad Habits and Begin a Healthy Lifestyle*. Now York: Center Street; 2005.

the "human" to the machine. It was actually Freud, much earlier, who viewed the organism not as passive but active, not simply a responding machine, but one that generates and creates its world based on what it feels and what it wants. Not that I want to extol its virtues unnecessarily, but is there any activity more than running that reminds us we are active individuals? Do we not indeed refer to what we are doing as "activities" rather than "passivities?"

Of course to Freud, much of what we want we don't actually know that we want, and so it remains to therapy to help us discover it. If we choose to. Which we don't always do, because we resist knowing. If I come to know that what I really want is not to succeed, or to lose my money so someone else will have to take care of me, or to injure myself so I won't have to take my licensing exam, or to starve to death so I won't have to worry about how I look, or to marry my mother or to kill my father or to give myself pain because I'm guilty of having those thoughts, or to return to the remembered bliss of childhood, or to return to the horrors of childhood so I can get even with all those responsible, then I may not be better off. But too bad. The truth, if anything can, will set you free.

Adding to the dilemma is that our primitive desires produce inevitable conflict with the world. Because the world is not so constructed as to facilitate our individual wants, they run up against (conflict with) society's constraints, causing us either to repress too many of them (exhibited by the typical neurotic) or act on them and get incarcerated in one institution or another (the typical psychotic). So we tread water, trying to negotiate between satisfying these wants or motives and fitting in with a society or civilization we need. For civilization is not the product of our most complete selves, as interpreted by those sociologists or political scientists or anthropologists who investigate its origins ("... to protect the common welfare, provide for the common defense, ensure domestic tranquility").

Freud's work, *Civilization and Its Discontents*, encapsulates in its title the price we have to pay to prevent the chaos that would result from a more primitive existence where each is literally out for his own self.

Taken a step further, these wants are often in conflict with each other as well. We want to take another piece of double chocolate fudge ripple cake with peanut butter praline ice cream, but we also want to stay healthy. We want to run off (escape) and be free, but we also want to stay within the comfort and bosom of our family. Life, to be ideally lived, according to Freud, must therefore invariably involve compromise. It's not the relentless pursuit of a single goal or manifestation of a single motive or fulfillment of the most important need, like achievement or friendship or even self-actualization, that Maslow put at the top of his hierarchy.[60] We can never assure ourselves that if some is good, more is better, because we must continually adjust our desires to fit in with other desires and the world.

Which takes us to the central question of why we run. Is it to achieve something, or is it to do something healthy? Is it to relieve tension and get rid of some problems, or is it a social activity designed to have us do something with compatible others? Is it to gain respect or acknowledgment from the world, or perhaps to show off in front of everybody? If those two million spectators do provide us an incentive to keep going up First Avenue and down Fifth, to break through the wall and come gliding past Tavern on the Green, then it can't be just me alone who was thinking (finally, after it had been anything but fun for so many months, so many runs, so many absent "highs"), "I like this, but enough of this." I loved it when they called my name, I did feel that parade was just for me—as my oldest son had described his own first marathon reaction. And I did want

---

60 In the famous Maslow pyramid, base needs (e.g., hunger) are at the bottom and each successive level must be fulfilled before going higher.

everyone to tip his hat, if not at my sentences (as Kafka was reputedly known to fantasize), then at my barreling to the finish line after running 26 miles. But I also felt, as indicated in the earlier chapter on social facilitation, that it wasn't quite genuine; that the few hours of honeymoon weren't going to last; that, while my name might have been distinctive, I'll bet you say that ("Looking good, Ethan") to everyone. Wants are complicated. Wants are conflictual.

Discovering the motives for why people do this is of particular interest since, as I've been at pains to describe, running is often painful physically, emotionally, and interpersonally. I had the advantage when I was training of not living with anyone and of getting great support from those who cared about me, most notably my kids. But I've also indicated how significant they were in motivating me in the first place, along with my own desire to fight off being a voyeur and slipping into a rocking chair. Someone I barely knew, a full-time lawyer and father who I was told was a runner (it turned out he's done half a dozen marathons, including Boston), admitted without hesitation that he had done the first when he was turning forty as a protest over lost youth. I didn't offer my thoughts on 40 being "over the hill," considering all the hills there were yet to climb and that I was waiting for my Medicare card to arrive.

This fight against deterioration was certainly a common theme, as others responded to my simple question, "Why do you run?" with "to stay young … to stay healthy … to keep fit." There were other responses as well, representative of the questions above and prompting me to make some of the categorizations below, but it was also curious how many seemed quite vague. "I like how it makes me feel … I enjoy it … I don't know, I just need to … What kind of question is that? Why not?" So I needed to find a way to get beyond the obvious and possibly tap motives that weren't so apparent, even to the respondents themselves. I was sure they were there because for so many who have responsibilities including but not limited to work, the sacrifices and the impingements on time are quite real. It's no accident that running's proponents often glorify its benefits ("Thousands of ... creative thoughts and inspirations ... start oozing out ... {when you} put one foot in front of another"[61]) because they're overdefending against the possibility that, like any activity that takes away from family time, their loved ones might end up hating their preoccupation or ignoring them or calling them so self-involved. (Do divorce lawyers hear as the reason for filing not just "He ran off with another woman," but simply "He ran off too often"?) How lucky are those runners I see who can run *en famille,* pushing their strollers while circling the loop or tethered to the dachshund, each obviously earnest in purpose.

Many have constructed a test to get at motivation, one of the most notable being the TAT or "Thematic Apperception Test." Originally designed by psychologist Henry Murray, it consists of a number of cards depicting a scene, with the subject being asked to tell a brief story about what he sees. As on all projective tests, we assume that you will throw (literally, pro-forward, ject-throw) onto the screen or onto your perceptions or, in this case, into your story the basic themes of your personality. You examine the first card depicting a child with a violin, outside of whose window one can see children playing on the street. You tell a story that the boy is forced to play the instrument while he would rather be outside playing ball with his friends, but because he spends so much time practicing he grows up to be a successful concert violinist while his friends are still hanging out on the street. The examiner's interpretation is that you have a high need for achievement. The fact that the hero of your story (you) attains a distant goal through sacrifice is a confirmation of your wish to do just that.

---

61 J. Galloway. *Training Journal.* Atlanta, GA: Phidippides; 1998.

In one article on amputees, handicapped runner John Keith finished his account of running the marathon by saying the familiar "I feel like I could do anything. I really believe you've got to have goals when you're injured like this."[62] He's right, but they're not just for those who are missing a limb. The importance of having goals is certainly one of the more emphasized areas in sport psychology and, indeed, elsewhere.[63] Not for nothing are the objectives in hockey, soccer, football, and basketball to get it into the goal or across the goal line or between the goalposts. In business school, some graduates tell me, whether it's marketing or merchandising or finance, it seems to be all they talk about there as well. And if you've ever been trapped into attending academic meetings, workshops, or "retreats" led by administrators who all seem to have taken weekend degrees in obfuscatory and pretentious pedagogy, then you will emerge with "goals" and "objectives" (as if they were different) gushing from every orifice.

I reflect on this at the moment, for I must now push myself in writing as I did in running. Not just two miles (or pages), but three. The scheduling becomes all-important. Four days a week, at first, to get started, to get a routine. Then five, and sometimes six. First a half-hour, then three-quarters, then an hour. Go up slowly. Try for too much too quickly, and the attempt is similar to starting out too fast in the race. It's why we give up.

A major finding from the achievement-motivation research mentioned earlier is consistent with these observations. Shoot for the moon and you won't get there, but you'll have an excuse. You want the Nobel or Pulitzer Prize, fine; but strive for too much too soon and you'll get discouraged at the first

---

62 J. Macur. "On the Road to Recovery, a Lift from the Sidewalks of New York." *New York Times:* Nov. 7, 2005; p. F4.

63 E. Locke. & G. Latham, G. P. "The Application of Goal Setting to Sports." *Journal of Sport Psychology,* 7: 1985; pp. 205–222.

hamstring pull or brain cramp or rejection slip. So the motive to achieve is not as easily identifiable as one might think, and it has more to do with one's own set of goals and how one sets them than with anybody else's.

According to "goal-setting theory," goals should be specific, quantifiable, and realistic— that is, attainable. But the early work on achievement motivation also focused on changing goals, implying that there was a need to change once you either attained your goal or saw you weren't going to attain it. A writer on running, Monica Smith, recently told me how disappointed she was in her performance in the marathon of 2004, the last two miles being particularly "horrible." I had expected her to tell me she hadn't finished or took all day, but she said she had completed it in 3:40. But her second half was a good 30 minutes slower than her first, and that was the cause of her disappointment. In other words, she realized toward the end that her expectation (perhaps of a 3:25) wasn't going to be reached, and that so disappointed her that she thought the whole race a failure. My elder son expressed a similar sentiment after his fourth marathon, when he too became disappointed and wanted to stop when he saw he wasn't going to beat his previous time (he was all of four minutes slower). So not everyone is exhilarated after the run, because not everyone feels he or she has achieved something. It depends on what your goal was.

And here's another word of wisdom on goals, gleaned from my own experience. Add something to your original goal (lower time, longer distance) after you achieve it, but not when you're pursuing it. That, too, is a recipe for failure. Perhaps what these individuals thought, when they came out a little faster than they should have, is that they could do better than anticipated, that they were on track to keep up their early pace. The advice here, as most runners have heard, is to resist the temptation to do just that. I remember on one of my early long runs thinking I would do two loops of the park, and then decided to add two more (14 miles total) at the end. Those proved very difficult, for whatever reason. Since they weren't part of the normal six-mile loops, I had to retrace some of my steps, and it was a struggle. Had I originally aimed for those fourteen miles and pictured the route I'd be taking, it would have been different. In fact, I always find it interesting that no matter what distance I set out to run, I generally feel at the end that this was all I could do, whether it was thirteen or three miles. If you set out to write an essay of 1000 words and then think it better be 1500, it will be a lot harder than trying for 2000 and then merely completing 1500.

But there's a danger here too, making the whole area of goal-setting even more complicated. In many endeavors, there's a tendency to stay satisfied with an achievement that is more than you expected, when you might do still more. "Satisficing" is what it was originally called by investigators into risk-taking. "Let me just get even," the gambler or investor says once he's been losing. It may be fine if he achieves it, but it also may limit the extent of what he could achieve. It's easier to see this in a tennis match, where once a person gets on the board instead of being shut out, he's satisfied, he avoided embarrassment. He's lost, 6–3, he's been respectable, he avoided the feared 6–0. But the question remains whether he could have done something, once he came back from 5–0 down to 5–3, to keep it going. Did he do more than relax and alter his goal, thereby achieving less than he might have? I always felt, when running, that I never wanted to settle for less than I had planned; and to ensure that I wouldn't, I would keep going for a bit more, even if it was only .05 of a mile on the treadmill or two city blocks outdoors. Not that plans couldn't be changed once the weather or obligations interfered, but not too casually and not once it was started. Yes, I'll do three, not four, since I'm pressed, but that decision is made before going out the door. Otherwise I'm in danger of lowering expectations constantly, of doing what all those proud writers of "still single but looking" biographies proclaim they'd never do, of having to settle.

Previous research on running has yielded somewhat mixed results, so I designed my own questionnaire, briefly described below, with what's called "forced-choice" comparisons to ascertain motivation. But first let me take time to explain something of the origin of this, as it was a technique originally designed to yield a subject's hierarchy of motives as a more objective form of personality assessment. One of the problems with all of this attention to motivation, particularly that which is so unquestionably "goal-directed," is that it often lacks what researchers like to call "objective measures." Projective tests like the TAT may uncover a lot, but interpretations depend on the interpreter. One reader sees a complex arrangement of parts to reach a complex whole, and another sees dallying around (running around in circles, as it were). It is therefore no accident that more objective measures have been designed; in fact, one of them—the Edwards "Personal Preference Test"—was a derivative of the TAT and attempted to measure basic needs, starting with "achievement." Examples of some others were "order," "aggression," "affiliation," "dominance," and "sexuality." By pitting a description of each of these against each of the others, and asking the subject with which she agreed more —A) I would like to have as many friends as possible; B) I would like to achieve something of great significance—the test would result in a ranking of the individual's needs.

Based on the most common answers given to the earlier motivational question, I designed my own questionnaire and constructed a similar set of choices based on these six scales (note that there are five different "instances" under each heading):

1) Health—This was measured by "I run ... to keep my weight down; to lower the risk of certain diseases; to keep myself fit; to keep physically fit; for health reasons;"

2) Psychological—because "it gives me a feeling of competence or confidence; it's exciting; it relieves tension; I have to; it distracts me from my problems;"

3) Achievement—"to achieve something; to push myself toward higher goals; to improve my own time; because it gives me a sense of accomplishment; to see how well I can do;"

4) Social—"to socialize with others; to share an experience with others; to meet people; because I enjoy being with others doing something similar; to be part of the crowd;"

5) Exhibitionism—"to earn respect from others; so people will be proud of me; so people will look up to me; to be seen as doing something special; to show off;"

6) Competition—"because I like to compete with others; to improve my time relative to others; because I enjoy competing with others; to beat someone I haven't beaten before; to do something not everyone can do."

You will note that there is some obvious redundancy among the items, although an effort was made to keep them somewhat distinct, and some are general (for health reasons) and some specific (to lose weight). It should be apparent that one might be motivated by the general and yet not fit into the specific, but being too general would be more redundant. In Edwards' test, a measure of achievement was "doing something of great significance," but another was " ... like to write a great novel or play." Obviously, one could be a high achiever without wanting to be a writer (and I suppose the reverse is even more true).

As with any such objective test (they're called "objective" because the scoring is standard, markable by a computer, and not dependent on any scorer's interpretation), every effort is made to standardize and validate interpretations. However much one may disagree with what an individual item in an objective test might mean or signify, there is no possibility of discrepancies between scorers.

The particular scales were chosen, as indicated, to be representative and comprehensive, but also to make distinctions that aren't always obvious. "Seeing how well I can do" is clearly different from "Beating someone I haven't beaten before," but sometimes the distinctions between these measures of achievement and competition are finer (e.g., "Improve my own time" vs. "Improve my time relative to others"). Doing something "to be with others" is quite different from wanting their "respect." While the latter is certainly not equivalent to "showing off," it was considered a more subtle way of exhibiting your talents and thus could be so characterized. In fact, for some analytic purposes, the six scales were grouped into two: the first three (Health, Psychological, and Achievement) being considered "Internal" motives and the last three (Social, Exhibitionism, Competition), "External."

Before discussing results, let me offer a word about the evident limitations of such questions. As with any objective test, people can lie. Or, to be kinder, they may not know themselves sufficiently well to be able to admit to certain motives—particularly if they haven't been to therapy. One doesn't confess that he likes to show off. Wanting to be with people or to achieve are considered more socially acceptable. To many individuals, even whole segments of the population, admitting to psychological necessities like the need to relieve tension or to solve certain problems does not come easily, as doing so may be seen as a sign of weakness. Men, at least until recently, have been particularly loath to expose such needs, as it runs (is situated as to be) counter to the male ideal of being invulnerable, in control, the protector of others. Hence men are less likely to come willingly to therapy (they are still a minority); they tend to be the ones coaxed in or bribed or threatened. I've even heard therapists advocate more leniency with men's appointments, ostensibly because their schedules are not as flexible as women's (as if they were all airplane pilots or talk-show hosts), but in reality so as not to scare them off.[64]

Despite this disadvantage of the objective test, that one can better see and thus disguise what is being asked about, it is still widely used because of its greater reliability. The examiner presumes that even if initially guarded, subjects will gradually stop posturing. One way of trying to measure this is to ask the same type of question in a different way. On my inventory, I also went after motivation by simply providing a few empty lines for subjects to explain why they ran. By comparing these answers to those on the forced choices, reliability could be ascertained. This was accomplished by having a scorer for each "open-ended" response who was unaware of the other answers given (in fact, the forced choices appeared later on the back of the page and could be scored independently without confounding the results). Multiple classification of the answers was allowed when subjects gave more than one reason or a reason that could be scored as more than one—e.g., "I run to be around people and show them what I can do;" this would be scored as "social" and "exhibitionistic"—and then compared to the most common motive. If there was a tie, then both were considered. I don't want to get too technical here, but am explaining this in some detail as to justify my confidence that the results do tell us something.

---

64 Nevertheless (we hope), things seem to be changing as even the most "macho" among us have come to recognize (we hope) the value of opening up. Firemen and police have started their own therapy groups, or at least have become more agreeable to joining them when programs have begun. In New York after September 11, 2001, when many uniformed workers had some direct contact with Ground Zero and practically all knew someone who had died, psychological services were soon made available by various organizations and, slowly, attendance picked up.

In the vast majority of cases, some 75 percent, there was agreement between the subjective and objective responses. It could be argued, of course, that even in the open-ended response, subjects might be guarded—perhaps it is easier to say, "I do it for fun" than "I do it because I'm blindly ambitious and want to beat everyone I see and have discovered that if I persist long enough, I'll outlast most people and then I can laugh in their faces and think 'What do you have to say now, you smart alecks who used to make fun of me when I was plump in junior high school and always picked last for the kickball team?'" Nevertheless, it's also evident that when you're not selecting someone else's choices, there's less temptation, perhaps less thought given, to covering yourself up. This is why it's harder to lie on projective tests, since the material is more ambiguous. Who knows what you're revealing when you're asked to describe an indiscernible inkblot, or given a blank sheet of paper and asked to "draw oneself"? How much more guarded is one going to be when asked to agree or disagree with the statement "I often hear voices telling me what to do"?

Here, then, is a brief summary of the results:

Over 90 percent of subjects were scored "Internal" rather than "External" on their motivation source. This is statistically quite significant, considering the number (some 300) and variety of individuals queried. My assistants and I interviewed runners of both sexes, of various ages (18–82), of vastly different running experience, and from various parts of the country and Canada. They also were scored on "athletic identity." This concept came into use over a decade ago and was illustrated not only by whether people consider themselves athletes, but by whether they tend to pick associates who are themselves athletes, to talk about their athletics with anyone who'll listen, to get depressed if not engaged in their athletic activity, and to build a life or at least a day around their sport.

To complete looking at the results on motivation, we found

that within the "External" group there wasn't much variation among the sub-groups, although Exhibitionism tended to be chosen less often than "Social" and "Competition." But within "Internal," "Health" was chosen about 50 percent of the time, and "Psychological" and "Achievement" about 25 percent each. Regardless of gender or identity, younger runners tended to value achievement more than older, perhaps not surprisingly, since they may still envision themselves as becoming superathletes or breaking three hours in the marathon, while the older generation is happy to be able to get up those stairs, much less the Stairmaster.

Relationships among categories other than motivation were found, and since they're there, I'll ignore the chapter title and mention them briefly. The young (defined as "less than 40") tended to consider themselves more as athletes and, perhaps surprisingly, this was more true of women than of men. Or, put another way, as they grew older, women identified themselves less as athletes, presumably because of competing roles. Though one might ask why such competition is not true of men as well, the result is consistent with an informal observation made of numerous New York Road Race finishers. There seems to be a greater percentage of women runners in their 20s, but more men in each age group division, starting with the 30s. Have men become more conscious of their health as they grow older? Or more competitive? Or more achievement motivated? (Okay, I'm back to the chapter title.) Or have they simply more time than women? Or do they care more about health and psychological "stuff" once the other activities—career striving, perpetual socializing—dominating the 20s have begun to pall? But why, especially in this age of gender equality, should women in their 20s be any different? We await, as we say, further research.

When I asked numerous runners what they thought of this age and gender disparity, they were unimpressed. It made perfect sense to them. Women, who tend to join groups more than men, consider running a social activity, preferring to avoid the more common meeting places to choose an activity that they like doing and through which they stand a better chance of finding compatible partners. It is certainly true that of the 25 or so treadmills I see occupied at various times of the day and week in the gym (actually, in many gyms, since I made a habit of utilizing all the passes I could get—in the interest of research, of course—resulting in my becoming familiar with over 30 spots in Manhattan alone, over 50 in the boroughs, and over 65 in the tristate area), most of them are being tread on by women. The men, fewer in number, are there but in the other room, pumping iron and flexing their muscles. But ambivalence is evident as well, because many women also indicate that they hate being "hit upon" while they're running, notwithstanding the flexing of their own bodily overexposure, and tend to run out (escape) rather than "hang," even when there is a juice bar.

From the various other results of the study, I'll cite a few that seemed of particular interest. It became apparent that not everyone employs a constant strategy over the course of a run, particularly a long one, or the same strategy that they do when training or running. While many a runner said he likes to train alone, but (obviously) be with people in a race, so did many indicate that internal or external association or dissociation also varied, even within the same run. Sometimes, said more than a few, they paid close attention to their bodies, alert to signs of potential distress (internal associators); but after a time, once they "hit their stride," they'd find themselves in their own world, even referring to it as a "trance" (internal dissociation). And it also seems to be true that accomplished runners in a heavily competitive race pay a good deal of attention not just to their bodies, but to the runners around them (external associators). Hendrik Ramaala in the last half of the 2005 New York Marathon (you may remember it as mine) was constantly looking over his shoulder to see where others were—

particularly Paul Tergat, the eventual winner by 0.31 seconds. Jelena Prokopcuka, the womens' winner, remarked in her interview that she was so conscious of others that when she saw Susan Chepkemei, who was leading at the time, getting sick on the course, she gained confidence knowing that the illness might limit the Kenyan's ability to stay in front. In any event, the stars may run to their own inner drummers but they are paying attention and don't seem to escape pain by "tuning out" or dissociating (like me). When I asked Grete Waitz whether there were any particular difficulties in that first marathon she did in New York, for I remembered she had described what a unique experience it had been for her to go that distance after running much shorter ones in Norway, she answered that she had indeed found it extremely difficult to go beyond 20, that distance itself being totally new to her, but she managed by imagining that the last six were just the distance she regularly ran from her home to the mall. This is paying close attention to your inner runner (or, once again, internally associating).

The motive for looking closely at motives is—and I don't apologize to anyone for invoking Freud again—because they're central, as he considered them, to understanding personality. While I've shown in this study what many have concluded about the (loneliness of the) long-distance runner, that he's impelled more by inner than outer motives, we may also find as a corollary that those who run shorter distances or when they're younger or when they're less constrained by outer influences to admit it, pay significant attention to the outer world. Yes, they may be less competitive than tennis or basketball players. Yes, they may be less exhibitionistic than strippers or even actors.[65] Yes, they may be less social than dancers and partygoers. But nonetheless, they can be all of these.

---

65 Or, even more so, teachers. Freud suggested that anyone who chose a profession commanding the attention of others was motivated by the desire to take off his clothes in public.

Yes, do it for yourself; but don't be ashamed, social animal, if you've got an eye on the impression it creates. When asked how I did in my Big Run, I was pleased to see how many of the cognoscenti, rather than ask me my time, asked me if I was happy with it. And while I certainly was, adding some variation of my usual happy-finishing-in-December quip, it was nice that they recognized the achievement had to be defined by the mind of the achiever. But having said that, I also love the idea that I finished respectably, that those who knew my brief and torturous history meant it when they called the feat "amazing." I have stopped wearing the marathon shirt they gave us, but not too long ago. (When I was brandishing it at a bar two weeks after the event, and one woman asked me if I'd washed it yet, I naturally responded, "Never.")

When we absorb Maslow's wisdom about the hierarchy of motives that he erects, when he suggests that after we've taken care of those mundane survival needs and then the social needs that we can reach the pinnacle by attending to our creative, independent, self-actualizing needs, I become a bit unsure of how the lunatics, the truly independent who take no heed of others, invent their own moral codes, who speak only to themselves (while carrying cell phones as they run) are so distinguishable from these most-fulfilled individuals. Run for yourself, by all means. Do it for yourself, whatever it is. But be mindful of this world, please, where others not only, in Freud's sense, compromise us, but can even motivate us. "Do it," as Salinger's Zooey said long ago, "for the fat lady." She's sure to notice your runner's body under that souvenir shirt.

11

What Runs Through Your Mind— Cognition

$\mathbf{A}$s both an area of and approach to the domain of psychology (an academic distinction I needn't bother to make, but old habits die hard), cognition has gained prominence in recent years. On the one hand, it refers to the fields of thinking and perception and learning and memory that Behaviorists have problems accepting because they don't acknowledge anything's going on that we can't see or measure. But it also signifies a way of thinking which is as old as the Greeks (the root of the word, *cognitus*, refers to ways in which we "know" the world), and which distinguishes itself from the "affective," or emotional, approach taken by Freud and on which so much of the previous discussion of motivation and personality and abnormal psychology rests.

While nonagenarian Albert Ellis, in his dotage, may not have enjoyed the fruits of his laborious contribution as he should, according to reliable reports (there was a major dispute at his

Institute of Cognitive Therapy, which resulted in his not being able to practice there in the same capacity), it was primarily he and a few others who promoted the radical departure. If we're going to believe, as many were ready to discover, that neuroses characterize a good deal of the behavior of a good deal of the population, then, in typical American fashion, we're going to want to find a cure. But not one that requires years of lying down on the couch five times a week. Or even three times a week. Or even sitting up.

Ellis promoted the idea that it wasn't the awful event in our childhood that was causing our emotional disturbance, but rather what we thought about it. So while we cannot change the past event, we can change the cognition or belief. Yes, you were not given enough toys as a child. But instead of being angry at your parent for the deprivation you cannot change, you can rethink the whole sorry event. By rationalizing it away and saying it was a good thing? By forgiving them, for they knew not what they did? By telling yourself, "Get over it," or "Move on"? No, by changing your irrational belief. You're thinking "They should not have done that," or "This was awful," or "I'll never recover from such neglect." Only by getting rid of your "awfulizing," or your "shoulds" or your "catastrophizing," by changing these illogical beliefs to logical ones, will you be cured. "I would prefer it if they hadn't done such a thing" is designed to replace the others; and by believing it, the patient's intensity, hence the illogic, hence the extreme anger, dissipates. Just substitute an "I would prefer it if …" for any "I must," and the irrational becomes rational.

One route that a cognitive approach to sport therapy takes rests on discovering common irrational beliefs and replacing them with more logical ones, and I've made a list of these below. And since sport, of course, is only a mirror of or metaphor for life, if the disputing technique works for, say, hunting for the ideal socks, it should also work for hunting for the right job or "soul mate."

Consider, for example, the common practice of procrastinating. I'll start my (exercise program, diet, term paper, job hunt) tomorrow ... and tomorrow ... and tomorrow. Can we, acting as cognitive therapists, find the root of this, the assumptions that are both limiting and irrational?

1) I must always be at my best.

So you don't write the paper yet or approach the person from whom you fear rejection because you're afraid not just of failing, but of its being a catastrophe. Perfectionism is at the root of procrastination.

Waiting till you feel better may be a healthy form of preparation, but beware, since there'll always be a better time or occasion. Interminable delay is the obsessive's price for trying to get it perfect. When is it okay to proceed? After four or fourteen or forty stretches? And should you begin prematurely, you'll be in danger of disappointing. Hence,

2) I must not let my friends, teammates, family down.

Yes, it's nice when you really succeed in their eyes, when your supporters genuinely share your joy. But even having put the added pressure on myself to let everyone know what I was doing, I also knew they'd be there should I not finish or even not get to the starting line. (Would I pull a muscle in the hour before? Would I miss the bus? Would I get enmeshed in some bureaucratic entanglement before it starts because I wouldn't be listed? Would my chip fall off so my time wouldn't really count?) And consider the pressure on the elite runner, the Kenyan who must not let his countrymen down.

3) I must succeed (win). All the time.

When you give a commendable performance (get to the finals, finish in the top ten, win an honorable mention), are you disappointed not to have won the gold? Perhaps if you're

Michael Jordan or Lance Armstrong; but often, having been at the very apex produces pressure that is the cause of a downfall. How many go out at the very top? Okay, maybe Jordan and Armstrong. Just look at all those boxers who, after they've had their shining moments, come back thinking they're still the champ and get humiliated. Floyd Patterson, Roberto Duran, Mike Tyson, George Forman. Give it a rest. Go put your name on a grill.

4) I must always be fit.

I must never put on an extra pound. Fear of gaining weight makes you obsessive or anorexic. Or delusional. Your sixty-year-old body is not what it was thirty years ago, nor does it have to be. Even Grete Waitz, as she steels herself these days for quite a different battle against cancer, is able to enjoy a "fun run."

5) I must always look my best.

What better example of how running reorganizes priorities? After my second training run, I was dashing off to a reception and didn't have time even to change my socks and sneakers. I did stop at the Road Runners office to get out of my soaked shirt, slip on a tie, and do a quick something or other at the faucet that perhaps doubled as a French bath; but for the most part, after 20 miles in the rain (my first run taking over three-and-a-half hours), I was a bit disheveled. And when someone later pointed out the whitefish on my tie and cream cheese on my nose, I laughed. How fully unself-conscious this running had made me. I could always put on my makeup later for the up-front-and-personal TV interview.

6) I must always beat those I've always beaten.

Competition is a common motive, even if not foremost among average long-distance runners, but to insist on this is a recipe for failure. Remember, there are good days and bad days.

7) I must always be as prepared as I can, especially mentally.

It should be difficult for me, the psychologist, not to insist on the wisdom of this, but I don't. I believe in mental preparation, but also in forgiving yourself.

8) I must always keep a steady pace.

It's desirable and, if practiced, prevents burning out. But what's desired isn't a necessity. Sometimes you must simply slow down or even stop. You can pick up again. And when you do, you don't have to erase the time lost.

9) I'm not suited for this because I've never experienced a runner's "high."

This is quite possible. As I've indicated at various points, I never have. Some never get an "alcoholic" high either, they claim, but are we going to assume that's some deficiency too? Or that we may even have different criteria for establishing its existence? As my old philosophy teachers were fond of saying when confronting epistemological dilemmas, "How do I know that what you mean by heartburn is what I mean by heartburn?" We may be calling two quite different experiences by the same name, or the same experience by different names, because we can never really experience what the other is experiencing. So your "high" may be my "medium."

10) I'll never be a true athlete (or runner) because I'm never as committed to it as I see "real" runners are.

I remember thinking myself deficient because I was equivocating about joining a running group just at the beginning of my marathon training. It would be a forced discipline and I'd probably benefit, but I also knew it would be an unrealistic commitment since other parts of my life (teaching, therapy) would interfere. I had managed to adjust my running to my own schedule, but was this only an excuse to stay away from the commitment? I answered "no;" I smiled and waved when I occasionally passed the groups en route to their destination; I stopped beating myself up for not fitting somebody else's definition of "true" or "real," and reminded myself of the ontological and metaphysical and Idealistic (in Bishop Berkeley's sense) interpretations of multifaceted reality.

11) I should always feel great after the run.

Whatever happened to my endorphins? Don't I have them or exude them? Sometimes I feel lousy and tired and cranky and upset that I didn't have time to do other things. Sometimes I slip into the rest of my day and don't feel better able to deal with stress or relate to people or negotiate conflict. Instead of being energized, sometimes I'm exhausted or worried or flying off the handle. Relax. It's okay not to be relaxed. Do you always feel great after eating, after sex? We're complex human beings whose reactions are not just physiological excretions. Were we a bit more primitive, maybe we'd bounce up and down like a four-year-old at recess or a puppy on seeing its owner come home, but the higher up you go on the evolutionary scale, the less our responses are a matter of blind instinct (or endorphins). Now, if you never feel good after exercise, then perhaps you ought to think of another route to nirvana. Only a masochist persists in finding ways to continue suffering.

12) I should be able to figure out if I'm a morning or evening person, but there must be something wrong with me because I can't.

Sometimes I love the morning run and hate the evening, and sometimes it's the opposite. The model, even your model, doesn't fit all sizes. Or days. Relish your idiosyncrasies; you'll find them more interesting. Do you always want to make love at the same time, in the same place, in the same position?

13) The mind should be able to tell the body to keep going.

Oh, we hear so much about this—how it's not about the legs and lungs but rather the heart and spirit, and certainly the psychologist ought to subscribe to it. The second half of the marathon, says Bob Glover, is all about mental control. Jeff

Galloway says that athletes go when the "left brain" says stop. And yet, there is Kathryn Switzer commenting on the recent marathon, looking at Chepkemie falter toward the end and saying "It's such a shame when the mind tells the body to do something and the body can't." If it were that easy (forgive the continual sexual metaphor but, after all, this is psychology), would we ever be impotent? In fact, sometimes the more you believe that you should be able to do something, the worse it becomes.

14) I should be able to build on my past accomplishments each time.

If you get an "A" must you now always get an "A?" Sure, training in any physical activity emphasizes a "buildup." You ran X miles last week, so increase it this week by 10 percent. Raise the bar when successful. But no one reaches any goal progressively, like a linear graph with constant slope. There are hiccups, caused by everything from the vagaries of life to the very fatigue resulting from constant exercise. You're supposed to rest and recover, to slow down and regroup. And I'm not just talking about tapering during the last stretch of marathon preparation. I'm talking about doing a shorter long run the week after the longer one, about doing 32 miles the week after you've done 36. Build up, yes; but not constantly, or you'll break down.

15) I should be doing this for myself, not for others.

Having gotten away from exhibitionism, the pendulum swings too far the other way. It's always just for you? Once in a while, at least, you can admit to showing off. You want to look good not just for yourself, but to be admired. You want everyone to say, there goes X the runner, X the celebrity. Remember, there are distinct motives for running and not everyone's out there for better health or to relieve tension or to better themselves in some way. Plenty are doing it to compete with others, to be with others, to be respected by others. If you want to get rid of those motives, you belong in the Zen monastery, not in Central Park with 37,000 runners being cheered by 2,000,000 spectators.

16) I must always feel like doing it or I'm not committed enough.

So much of the time, it takes special resolve to get out the door. There is nothing wrong with you for not particularly wanting to subject your body to this pain or turmoil. If you always feel like doing it, you're exceptional, delusional, or trying to impress someone. One day my friend the musician decided to stop practicing, and he never did it again. We should all have such resolve.

17) While I may get slower as I get older, I should enjoy running more.

Perhaps, but not necessarily. It takes its toll on mind and body, and if you actually think you're improving each year, you're either exceptional or delusional or you're trying to impress somebody. (Yes, they're common diagnoses.)

18) We are designed by evolution and nature to be runners and if we don't keep at it, we're violating our nature.

We're designed to be couch potatoes as well. The body can adjust quite well to the relaxing or the strengthening to which it's accustomed. We're designed to be poets and chefs and musicians and tree climbers and lumberjacks, so don't make a necessity out of virtue. For those who do it and do it well, fine. For the rest of us, be yourself.

19) I must be doing something wrong because throughout my running history, I never learned anything about my instep or pronation or the crown of the road or right brain.

Join the crowd.

20) I'm not a real runner because I never do speed work or hill work or interval work and I don't know a fartlek from a bialystok.

You're wrong. The true runner is within you. If you're not in touch with your inner runner, it has nothing to do with fartleks. Find a running psychologist. If he doesn't cure you, he'll run with you. And do a lot of listening. And maybe talk once in awhile.

21) I should be grateful I can do this, even modestly.

Yes, we look at all those people out there handicapped in some way, either because they're amputees and running in wheelchairs or because they've got different body types or metabolisms or grew up in lousy neighborhoods. Yes, count your blessings; but no, don't feel you have no right to complain about someone leaving you or not showing up or bumping into you on the track because there are worse things. Our feelings are not based on calculations from global perspectives that reveal our minimal place in the grand scheme of things. They're based on things more immediate, so immediate that we experience pain and delight on such a small scale that we still seek the latter and avoid the former. Most of us.

Having compiled this list, it seems only fitting to introduce a few rational thoughts compiled from the experience of running. Granted, as you will see, there are considerably fewer here, but then the lists reflect the relative amount of irrationality and rationality in the world, generally.

Rational thoughts:

1) I've never had a moment of inspiration while running, despite what the gurus say.

2) I'm as fast as I'll ever be.

3) Once my body starts running, it doesn't want to keep running. It wants to stop. Despite Newton or thermodynamics or inertia. A body in motion tends to want to stop.

4) When I take a nutritional energy bar or sip of a sports drink, I want to eat and drink more. I don't want to run.

5) Whenever I start to list the benefits of exercise, particularly running, I start listing the costs. And guess which comes out ahead?

6) The longest journey begins with a single step. And ends with strained IT bands, strained relationships and destroyed knees.

7) When I don't feel better after running a mile, I run two. When I still don't, I walk. When I feel worse, I buy ice cream and watch the History Channel.

8) If you don't feel great at the finish, don't start.

9) There is only the slightest difference between doing well and doing poorly. If for you it's shaving 30 seconds per mile and you can't accomplish it, lower your expectations.

10) If there are over 100 definitions of "run," there are at least that many different ways to do it. Don't accept any definition of it other than your own. And if you can't embrace one, find another dictionary.

Another well-trodden avenue along the cognitive approach to sport psychology involves visualization. No single concept in the field gets referred to more than this one, and it is clear it has some value. But visualization has been latched onto, I think, because there's a relative dearth of other empirically proved concepts, because it's easy to imagine (or visualize), and because its application to other areas of life is promising. But not everyone knows that the concept itself is derived from the cognitive theorists who, early on, conceived of it as a therapeutic strategy. The empirical groundwork is less certain than the theoretical promise, the latter being due to the bias we all have to base our theories on something physical. There's some talk in the literature about the left and right brain functions, about trying to inspire right-brain or creative functioning, and how running does that.[66] But it's simply a feeling and a wish that is being conveyed. Unless we conduct what at one time was called "split-brain research," we really don't know what's going on in there.

This is also true with so-called neurolinguistic programming. The argument goes that if we repeat something in our head enough times, then we etch pathways in our nervous system in much the same way that ice skating down a particular route will form a groove into which we can then more easily slide—or trip if we come at it from another angle. But since no one has been able to walk or impel their way down these well-worn paths, we really don't know what the physiological manifestation of such repetition really is, at least in our inner rather than the outer world.

Nevertheless, visualization has been promoted as an important phenomenon, and it does seem to work to a certain extent. There is talk of it in some health circles; I once worked for a quasi-religious organization that regularly did a visualization exercise, encouraging elderly people every week to form a mental picture of a desirable state, like reduced disease cells, and members felt better and swore by it. And one finds in certain meditative exercises that there's an emphasis on constructing such mental pictures, for example, as one goes through the various yoga positions.

In sport, there's been much talk of it and anecdotal evidence that it works. The basketball player who pictures his foul shot going just over the rim, the tennis player who pictures his serve falling into the box or even that portion of the service box for which he is aiming, the golfer who pictures the ball falling into the cup, the baseball player who imagines the ball he hits going over the fence, the diver who rehearses her ambitious feat in her head before walking to the edge of the board, even the weight lifter picturing the bar above his head

---

66 Galloway comes to mind.

—all report greater success from their efforts. Aerial skiers stand poised, taking ten deep breaths and visualizing a successful flight, before they take off. Ice skaters are told to picture the figure "8" before they go out there, and one accomplished skater told me that years later she still experiences in her whole body the sensation of accomplishing her "figure" when she reconstructs it in her mind.

Controlled studies that test this kind of "imagery," even when successful, don't yield conclusive results. For one thing, one has to wonder whether it's not just the calming, easy atmosphere that is producing the beneficial effect, rather than the construction of the actual picture. Visualization is not always distinguished from other kinds of mental rehearsal, and individuals certainly have different definitions of what it means to visualize and apparently different capacities for doing it.

Some time ago, psychologists, particularly those concerned with memory, focused on the capacity that a small minority had for what they called "eidetic" imagery. This referred to the ability to re-create in one's mind the picture that was no longer in front of one, with all its many details. Show a street scene to an eidetic imager and she will, a moment later, scan the background of the picture to make out what the letters were on the sign of the shop. Perhaps this is what we mean by someone's having a photographic memory. Some accomplished word-players, such as Scrabble champions, have apparently been able to "memorize" all eight-letter words in the dictionary encyclopedically (or dictionarily) because, once they've seen it, they can then scan each page in their heads. Gestalt psychologists some time ago paid particular attention to the "afterimage" of a picture flashed to subjects on a screen to see what part this played in our perception of events. A tennis lineswoman I know reports that she is much better with her calls if the umpire gives her an extra half-second to decide if a ball was in or out (some who don't know or trust her are a bit too peremptory in their overrules) because she can then, even in that brief moment, play the shot back in her mind, her own instant replay, to see if it grazed the line.

The imaging capacity does vary among individuals, and recent investigations have looked at how different sensual modalities may interact with the purely visual. Is there a kinesthetic kind of imagery (Is that what my ice skater was doing 25 years later?), or a dynamic kind where one experiences her perception in more than one sensory modality? Some research suggests that men do more dynamic picturing and women are better at the purely visual. For some the past may be harder to conjure up than a visual fantasy of the future—are your sexual fantasies about people you once knew or hope to know? All of this may explain the difficulties in experimentally validating the phenomenon. Moreover, some conceive of the process as being more one of anticipation rather than of just visual acuity, a process that is known to have beneficial effects.

So on the one hand, runners may be advised to visualize the course that they will go through, particularly on a long run, but are also told—and I was one who followed this advice—actually to go to the course to familiarize themselves with its various twists and turns, the surrounding scenery, the neighborhood. And in the two weeks before my own marathon, I did just that in two different but significant portions of the 26 miles. First one son took me over the Queensboro Bridge in both directions, a particularly steep and lonely portion of the course that comes at the 15-mile point. When I got there during the actual race, and started a gradual climb for about a mile, I was not only unperturbed, but I could provide information to a couple of Midwesterners running close to me, looking bewildered and asking "What is this?" I had become the guide. Yes, First Avenue is coming up. Empire State Building next, then Chinatown, then the Staten Island Ferry. Almost. But I knew where I was, and that helped.

Yes, cross your bridges before you come to them.

The other equally familiarizing and valuable training run I did came two weeks before the marathon, when I was advised by my other son to join a group that was running the last ten miles of the course. It started right over that Queensboro Bridge and extended into upper Manhattan and the Bronx, and then circled back through Harlem, Fifth Avenue, and eventually the last 2½ miles in the park. This is Central Park, where I had actually practiced many times, running many loops in many different directions, and done most of my long runs of 16, 18, and 20 miles. But on this particular occasion, exactly foreshadowing the last and most taxing part of the race, it was quite different. For one, I had never run the last part of the actual route, exiting the park at 59th Street, running along the wide street known as Central Park South, and coming back in at Eighth Avenue to finish the last few hundred yards. It covered the territory where German Silva in 1992 made his infamous wrong turn and ended up almost losing (he won by two seconds, the closest margin of victory until this year's 0.31 second differential). And while running it in the race was not exactly the same as starting out from the 16-mile point, it still helped because I knew, I could picture, I anticipated what it was going to look like. It certainly helped me through the last six miles, having never before run more than 20, and perhaps enabled me to scale the "wall" which had been looming as a potential obstacle for so long.

There are plenty of things one can visualize, of course, besides the actual run. The scenery, the crowds, the cheers (audibilize?). The touch of the water or Gatorade as you pick these up from the stations (tangibilize?). For some, playing the highlight reel of your own running biography is a way of helping you along. Recall how you looked or felt when you did your best time in that half-marathon. Picture yourself coming across that finish line. Imagine the runners you were passing as you came close. It helps to anticipate the difficulties or obstacles as well, perhaps hurdling them so as not to be thrown by them in actuality. There are runners who will be passing you, perhaps even bumping you as they do. There will be a mess at those water stations, as people cut you off, as cups are not quite ready or spilled. The ground will be littered with these cups and (now I know, so bear it in mind, future New York Marathoners) huge yellow Sponge-Bob Square Pants things, so you may have to dance an Irish jig to avoid being sucked up by them at mile 19 or 20.

In other areas of life, perhaps in all, anticipation and visualization of the encounter helps. We sometimes "role play" in therapy, a perfect example of trying to reduce anxiety through anticipation. One of the best pieces of advice I received for preparing for graduate-school comprehensive exams—the most significant step toward the Ph.D., the one requiring at least a couple of years of preparation, and for which there was a reading list of over 200 titles—was to discover in which room they were holding it. "Go there beforehand, look it over, pick out your seat if you can," I was told. I did. And while sitting and writing for twelve hours over two days was a marathon in itself (and this was long before I had thought anything about sport metaphors), I survived. The environment being familiar, the initial anxiety was soon dissipated, so I could quickly start wrestling with the real problems on the paper rather than my own doubts.

Preparing oneself mentally can be accomplished in another way if we extrapolate from the experiments on "priming" from Gladwell's *Blink,* cited earlier.[67] If you devise a verbal task for people, such as rearranging certain words to form a sentence ("sky the seamless gray is"), and these sentences each have a word denoting a certain characteristic (old, gray, wrinkled), then people who leave the testing room actually act (by walking more slowly) in a manner consistent with that characteristic. Controlled experiments using words connoting aggression

67 M. Gladwell. *Blink.* New York: Little, Brown, & Co.; 2005 (p. 53).

or cooperation demonstrate something similar. The subjects have been primed.

Wouldn't it then follow that if we do "young word" priming, if we verbalize rather than visualize "fast" or "smooth," we'd have an easier time running? It sounds terribly simplistic, but if "gray" makes us walk more slowly, then a "finish line" mantra may get us there more quickly. We don't actually have to pin a piece of it to our shirt—something I mentioned that my colleagues on the "Psyching Team" were prone to advocate—we can carry it in our head. If the picture of our best performance facilitates another, why not suggest, particularly to the less visual and more verbal, that the words signifying all that we want may do the same. "Young," "fast," "happy,"—I'm on my way. I'm going to have a nice run.

It occurs to me that I now have an explanation for why only some distractions I've tried while running have been of benefit when I'd been thinking that simply any would, that dissociation helped escape the pain. I counted the machines at the club where I'd exercised. Hard work, yes, but successful. I counted the number of days since I'd given up my nightly cigar. A success story, a testimony to endurance. But when I started making a mental list of all the women who had left me, I couldn't get through it and it was harder to scale those hills. So a note of caution. Don't visualize or verbalize failures.

And another note of caution before naively talking ourselves into scaling every mountain. It's quite possible that if we simply recite those pleasant words, we'll reject them and they'll have no effect. We don't simply want to follow advice (therapy) that is too directed. It gets resisted. We need to come up with it ourselves. The subjects in the priming experiments didn't know they were being primed. We need to sneak it in there a bit. Otherwise the "positive thinking" crowd would be totally successful. If they were, we'd all have "positived" ourselves long ago into blissful eternity.

12

Running in Place—
Perception

We hear a lot from sports pundits abut the importance of "focus," or how no one concentrates as well as Andre Agassi or Phil Michelson, but do we really know what this means? Seeing the ball so well? Keeping something in mind? (The immediate goal? Getting to the next quarter-mile? The long-range goal? Getting to Tavern on the Green when you're on the Verrazano Bridge?) As I've indicated in various places, particularly the chapter on "motivation," the importance of goals is stressed, perhaps overly stressed, throughout sport psychology, and I don't think the kind of concentration referred to here has anything to do with goals. In fact, it may be antithetical to it. It has to do with being in the moment, a term that actors and humanistic therapists use a great deal, and which captures something of where the perceptual mind is when it's truly focused. And this indeed may be when things "flow" as well, the term originally used by Csikszentmihalyi to indicate a condition of creativity in various endeavors.[68]

---

68 M. Csikszentmihalyi. *Flow: The Psychology of Optimal Experience.* New York: Harper and Row; 1990.

When Roger Federer seemed to lose concentration in the middle of his final match with Lleyton Hewitt at the 2004 U.S. Open, he later admitted it must have been at the point where he started picturing himself receiving the trophy. So much for that kind of visualization. And how apt a description and lesson for the runner. How can we get ahead of ourselves, the Zen Master might ask, when we always are where we are? Very easily. Getting too far ahead of ourselves is precisely what we can do mentally, and that's dangerous. What, then, does it mean to be "in the moment?"

When my younger son was five, we went to see *Return of the Jedi*. He, who had never managed to sit still for anything longer than four-and-a-half minutes, now sat entranced for a good two hours and fifteen minutes on the edge of his movie-theater seat, unblinking, mouth agape. When the credits appeared, he turned to me and fairly bellowed, "That was the best movie I saw ever ..." (He had previously seen four, each very much in installments) "... It was so good, I can't remember anything in it." That confession seemed to capture what being "in the moment" means. You're so immersed in the present that you're not registering anything for later recall. In fact, when therapy is conducted as it should be, I think something very similar transpires. How often do people begin a session by asking where we left off, in effect trying to get me to tell them something about our last meeting because they can recall nothing. How often are they unable (not simply unwilling) to share with others what indeed has taken place in that room, because no traces of that flowing, immediate experience persist?

The athlete who does attain his "high" (not from personal experience, mind you, do I refer to it), or one who feels those juices flowing or who is in the "zone," is similar to the musician, actor, ballet dancer, or even stand-up comic who seems to be magically coordinating his movements to the rhythms of the world, not thinking about what he's doing but reacting to his muse, if one wants to invoke a poetic metaphor. That this can be true of something as seemingly cognitive and verbal as the comedian's work is all the more remarkable, but the spontaneity of the talented improviser is evidence that even here something seems to be happening automatically. Can the athlete really be on automatic pilot?

Were any endeavor so susceptible, it would seem to be a solitary, repetitive activity like running. For no matter how "focused" that tennis player is, how is he able to remember the score? Not all the time, of course, as anyone who's ever played a match knows, for we all at some point lose it (and some of us over the age of 30, as one partner of mine always reminds me, a little more often than others). But, for the most part, we can recapture the last few points to remind us of where we are. And considering all those other variables of which we must keep track, doesn't it imply we're not simply going with the flow? The tennis player must know which side of the service court to be on and when to change sides and where to turn to find the last errant ball (those with ballboys are different). Once in a while I've gotten up from the bench after the minute changeover and realized to my chagrin as I got to the baseline that I'd forgotten my racquet. Now were I really in the flow, this would happen more often. It was so good, I can't remember what state (New York? Delusional?) I'm in.

What is apparent from all this—but is rarely formulated—is that, quite simply, there is a "front" of the mind and a "back" of the mind. Gestalt Psychology made use of this concept of the perceptual field in talking about "figure" and "ground." When we look at anything, the eye focuses on part of the scene (figure), and while we can see the rest, it's in the background. If I focus, I tell my students in the front of the classroom, I can still see the back row, but it's out of focus. And vice versa. It's what we see in the camera's eye when we focus. Those ambiguous figures that are usually captured in Psychology 101 text-books (vase or two profiles, old woman or young woman) illustrate the idea that the focus can change, and in these cases so dramatically that the entire percept is radically altered. We're familiar with the "Rashomon" effect (after the movie detailing how different perspectives radically altered the picture that all sincere reporters painted of an event) or the blind men and the elephant, each perceiving through touch a different object because of where they were standing and what part they were feeling.

But feeling has a more important and abstract position in the perceptual world, and can help explain why ten eyewitnesses to an event all report something different. Our feeling toward the event or toward the person in the event can, in Gestalt terms, serve as a context in which the percept operates, or in other words can "color" what we see. Do I love her because she's beautiful or is she beautiful because I love her? My love (or hostility or anger or prejudice against women) makes her seem quite different from anybody else. It is not simply those projective tests that assume and consequently prove that your perception is indeed your "projection;" for it is not simply because it is a "defense mechanism" that our own characteristics determine or at least influence how we view another being—that what Peter tells us about Paul tells us more about Peter than about Paul—but because so much of what we see says more about the subject than about the object. When I'm in love, the whole world looks appetizing, and all those children playing in front of me are so adorable and energetic and interesting. When depressed or angry, it's all quite something else. How come everyone (not just Seinfeld characters) hands out those pictures of the newborn, sincerely believing how "gorgeous" the little tyke is? Except the ones who aren't the proud parents.

So when do you forget the score? Less when you're winning. Or even who won the last point? When it's you who have lost it.

When one talks of being so focused, it cannot mean that everything else is not seen, but it does mean that the contrast is marked. Conversely, if one is not focused, there is no or little contrast between figure and ground, so everything becomes a distraction, every alternative seems possible, and choice becomes difficult or arbitrary. Sometimes, when I concentrate so hard on the words as I am spilling them out, when I am quite in focus, I will actually misspell some basic ones (I just did so two sentences earlier, writing "scene" for "seen") because I'm not even paying attention to anything but the sound of the word in my mind's ear. Maybe that makes me an auditory person, but for the moment, I'm glad to have at least that, some focus.

The runner's focus, if not necessary, is certainly important but also more attainable, since there's probably less that needs to be counted in the back of one's mind. Miles run? Yes, but unless you're doing an ultramarathon, that's a lot less of a task than a tennis score.

A more vivid example of this "back of the mind" phenomenon would be recognized by anyone who's ever played tennis on public courts. I devoted a whole chapter to this once, unabashedly referring to it as "how to get your balls back." "Thank you," your court neighbors scream, as soon as their "Wilson 1" enters the perimeter or parameter of yours. While your "Penn 2" sits there through rally after rally as they're either oblivious to it or cannot yet be disturbed. There may well just be a degree of self-involvement taking place (perhaps particularly so in the callous Big City) that can possibly explain, even when it can't justify, this kind of behavior. Those in cars feel it more often, when they're about to pull out of a parking space and the truck double-parks in front of them, ignoring pleas or horn. And the tow truck, as I walk back that mile through the city streets from the court, completely blocks my path, so bent on his mission is the tower. Are those tennis neighbors hostile or just oblivious? Can you be so wrapped up in your own activity as to be unaware of everyone else's? Not that it justifies anything, but with the concentration so great, sometimes it happens. More often, I can't help believing, there's that awareness in the "back of the mind," which just isn't ready to march forward. They see, but of course they're just busy with something else. Like the double-parked truck.

So what about runners? Is it possible that this is one area where self-absorption is permitted? That except for the slight problem of passing other runners, and perhaps not having enough room to do it, runners can get away with being oblivious because there's absolutely no reason why they have to be keeping track?[69] They are like Timothy Gallwey's "Inner Tennis" or "Inner Golf" or "Inner Volleyball" crowd: able, apparently, to pay simple attention to the rhythm of the universe, to say to themselves "bounce, hit," without worrying about the shoulder-turn or follow-through or knee-bend because such thinking just impedes progress. In running, you can get into that trance, you can solve life's pressing problems, you can get angry in fantasy at your boss or spouse or mother-in-law, you can play back all those wonderful home movies of your past because your hypnotic state is not generally going to interfere with your social responsibilities.

And for all I know, being in a kind of trance is what got me through my marathon without undue duress. It is not inconceivable that what I experienced is what Milton Erickson, a unique therapist, tried to induce in his patients. He talked of

---

69 Although nothing like the problem of passing pedestrian walkers; or double-strollers; or single strollers; or ambling, oblivious couples; or three-wide families, leaving half-a-person room between each. But don't you dare "break the (invisible) line" connecting them, or you're committing a sidewalk felony.

a variety of hypnotic trance called cataleptic levitation, a kind of step-by-step (what better example than running?) introduction to an altered state of consciousness. He even suggests going over the alphabet in your head to induce one, and I think of all the number games I would play to get me through the pain, to dissociate.

Of interest also is that Erickson introduces "external" and "internal" personality styles; and almost parenthetically, in talking of the different meanings that certain words have in English compared to other languages ("left," for example—an important difference to realize when treating patients from other parts of the world), he mentions the manifold meanings of "run" (the only other person I've seen do this) and some of the anomalies (the road's running "uphill" and "down," when it stands still).[70]

There were in my marathon aftermath a few joint problems for a few days, but not really that much more than usual. (One of the advantages of being the aged runner is that the aches and pains upon awakening are not that novel.) No terribly sore feet, no blisters, none of the common toe or breathing concerns. With all the emphasis I've placed on the runner's—particularly the urban runner's—need to look out for those strollers and runner-unfriendly pedestrians, the Marathon, being free at least of those obstacles (as indeed, are most races), may have permitted, if not quite the Csikszentmihalyian "flow," if not even a significant degree of fun, a release from worry about flowing right into a Con Edison manhole. Did I sweat in training, as they say, so I wouldn't bleed in battle?

Yes, if runners can afford to be oblivious in many circumstances to the world around them, they also prove to be a

---

70 J. Zeig. *A Teaching Seminar with Milton H. Erickson (Annual Progress in Child Psychiatry and Child Development).* Philadelphia, PA: Brunner/Mazel; 1980.

hardy group, disturbed less by the impediments of the environment.[71] They go out there because whether they're "inner" or "outer" directed, they're able to find or create a world in which they can do their own thing magnificently.

So as Malcolm Gladwell points out, sport is often about the "flow," how too much analysis leads to paralysis. And how does this apply to the urban runner, not quite frolicking amidst those ospreys near the brooks of Colorado? Perhaps it's the idea that you can be conscious of things without knowing you're conscious of them, an essential idea in *Blink.* I'm aware of the hidden driveway coming up or the pedestrian more attuned to her cell phone than the approaching runner or the cab not about to stop, so automatically my head turns, my arm goes up, I announce, "on your left." It's not a high-speed police chase, but it does contain that characteristic of having one's perceptual apparatus quite attuned.

And yet, this may also be why I find I must keep that pen with me as I run these days, lest a transient thought vanish. My present awareness has become so focused that, like my son, I won't remember anything. Sometimes it happens even as I write that the very act of putting one thought down, while I get another, prevents my remembering the second.

But don't underestimate the power of the pen. It also, by accident or design, allows more to come in. As I approach the net to jot something down, I hear on the adjacent tennis court a player explain to his partner what he was doing after he "hit the wall." I look up with curiosity and realize from what he's now saying about lifting his head too soon, that he must have said, after he "hit the ball." When I first started writing this, I walked into the library and "saw" my previous book, in its green cover, on a table next to the adjacent computer. This

---

71 On the first blustery day of December, winds blowing at 20–30 mph, there was no one on the very available park tennis courts but my partner and me, but I passed scores of runners.

would have been quite remarkable since, aside from copies in libraries and bookstores and those with which I've personally been familiar, I only once, on the subway years ago, discovered it in the hands of a stranger. And as I pass a coffee shop with a sign in its window saying, "We now have more lattes," it being Chanukah, I think it says "... latkes."

It's a phenomenon known as the apperceptive mass, although it has relevance to some areas of social psychology as well. Why is it that ever since I started running, so many others have been running as well? Do I have so much influence? And why are there so many new running shops? And particularly, now that I've run the marathon (albeit a relatively short time ago), the number of runners on the streets, in the park, by the walkways has clearly tripled. I see them everywhere, at all times of day and night, of all ages, in all kinds of gear. And when did the City redo all the streets and make every other one of them so much hillier? Somehow, these slight upgrades in the sidewalk were not there before.

Now that you've bought a car, has the city government installed more meters and "No Parking" zones? Now that you have a baby, are there more "snugglies" and strollers on the street? As our relationships serve as context for our perceptions, so do our experiences, particularly those which required a significant investment. To the social psychologists, the heightened awareness is a result of trying to reduce the cognitive dissonance that would accrue were the choice we made a poor one. We not only notice the other Volvos on the street once we purchase one, we're also likely to talk to the other owners, to compare notes on how good the mileage is and how much pick-up the engine has. (This is particularly true when the choice we made was a difficult one because our other option, the Toyota, was almost selected. It was a toss-up.) So we form Volvo fan clubs and go on the Internet to share Volvo love stories. Buy a computer, and you become invited or kidnapped into the *World of Apple,* the *Apple Journal,* the newest proud branch of the Apple tree.

But to the psychologist of perception, we are simply alerted to that object or activity which is now prominent in our consciousness. Now that running and aging are apparently uppermost in my own, I see ads on hip replacement and gastroesophageal reflux remedies and prostate pills. How do you, without resorting to paranormal phenomena, explain the fact that just two minutes after you've thought of a person you haven't seen in six months, there he is coming around the corner? Here's how. It's likely that there are legions of instances where you think of someone and this doesn't happen, or they might be there but you haven't seen them, but because you did, in effect, arrange your mind to be prepared for this, you pick him out of the crowd. We see what we're programmed—by fantasy, by motive, by experience—to see.

So I've been noticing runners. There are lots of them. Maybe I'll talk to them and join running clubs and share running stories, not so much because I'm in love with this so-called sport (albeit I may be the exception, for there appear to be plenty of others who are), but because I must now prove that it was worthwhile, particularly having invested so much into it. I could have been playing tennis. Perhaps I should have been playing tennis. Why was I spending all this effort on running? I must prove running is good.

And what if you now notice other things about running? Like how many runners there are out there who are slower? This, too, may be a function of the same need to reduce dissonance. If everyone's faster, I'm reminded of reasons I shouldn't have done it. That wouldn't be good. I'm not really a runner. Yes, I am. Look at how many slower ones there are. You think that didn't matter the last three miles of the marathon when I found myself passing people? It was just the kind of phenomenon that made this activity worthwhile (even though I was barely aware of it). And had I been walking, would that have made it a failure? Hardly. Look at how many others there are. It's perfectly legitimate.

And by the way, if you think the god of competition is always out there spurring us on to such self-justifications, you're right. Because wherever you go, you're likely to meet Socrates on his way back. Did a 3:40 marathon? My brother just did 3:30. Run your third? My father, who's approaching 70, just did his 25th. And as I left my building, sporting for the fourth day in a row my New York Marathon souvenir jacket, there within half a block was someone wearing, of course, a Boston Marathon one. And when I attended the first meeting on Sport Psychology at the American Psychological Association Convention last year, who is the author being honored? The compiler of the definitive bibliography (bibliography, no less!) on the Psychology of Running.

13

Being Overrun by Knowledge— Learning and Memory

Have you trained? It's the question I heard most often when I actually told people I was planning to run the marathon. With great trepidation would I confess my intent, you may remember, because announcing intentions offends the gods, who will then humble you. But yes, I had to admit, I trained. Not obsessively, but closely enough. I had followed the *New York Road Runners' Guide* or outline or website hints. No classes, thank you; I had too many reservations, some of which I referred to in the last chapter, and not enough stretching and nutrition-attention and massaging. But I had run.

I had begun—if it was only two years ago, it seems like an eternity; if it was already two years, it seems like yesterday— proud to reach a quarter of a mile. By the time the marathon date was in sight, I was running five times a week on average, managing a modest 15–20 miles total. When I started paying closer attention to the "buildup" countdown, I was gruesomely reminded of the wisdom behind stretching exercises, which I always ended up pretty much ignoring. How am I ever going to do 40 when I haven't come close to 30? So to counter my own oppositional tendencies (they're present, sometimes, after the age of two), I forced myself to begin the more-or-less official routine 24 weeks ahead, scheduling those all-important long runs on Sunday (and wondering if that was permissible, since the schedule called for Saturday, but I had to take a few liberties). I missed one day because of a trip out of town and made up for it Monday. While this threw my schedule off a bit, I didn't want to be obsessive or let a slight variation alter the big picture. Throughout that day, though, I did feel guilty until I got back, so to speak, on track.

I had even begun listing those long runs months ahead, starting at six, eight, and ten, not in exact sequence, but ultimately getting to my 16s and 18s and three 20s. It was adjusted for a couple of races, a tennis tournament or two, that trip away and another. I couldn't manage more than the "Running Psychologists" annual 5K at the convention in Washington, but I managed to get in my eleven on another trip to Montreal. So yes, I kept to it, even in strange picnic-and-dog surroundings with narrow paths and plenty of bicycles and even cars at some point. It almost made me feel right at home. I also managed my only fall on funny, slippery, well-hidden rocks, and could only estimate distances; but by then I was afraid to veer too much from the schedule for fear of losing "fitness," so I finished it.

Yes, I was able to say I'd trained.

But I always wondered where, literally, the training went—if my muscle fibers were twitching differently, you could have fooled me—where was the so-called fitness? And was this so-called training enough? Years ago, Thorndike introduced two laws of learning: the law of practice and the law of effect. The former, however, which is what mere training emphasizes, didn't hold up to experimental scrutiny. In other words, doing something over and over wasn't sufficient to incorporate it into your system; it had to lead to some beneficial effect, some reward. In his book, Governor Huckabee recognizes that when he succeeded in doing something he wanted, such as running his long run, he would need to reward himself for doing it. In my case, I rarely did (and running surely, in my case, wasn't its own reward) because I never let myself be sure I was making progress.

In fact, I couldn't help thinking that if I took more than a day off in those last couple of months, I'd soon be back where I started, no running remnant left. I was assured this would not be, that somehow my body remembered and, critics of Thorndike notwithstanding, I wanted to believe this was true. And yet, I also needed to be sure this actually worked, because with all we know about learning and memory, it would be nice to give some substance to what this sport or any sport's being largely "mental" really means.

Some call it "neurolinguistic programming," a popular term these days for what goes on in the body and used particularly by those, as discussed in the previous chapter, who delineate the physiological effects of visualization. You're actually etching something in those … what? Cells? Neurons? Synapses? The brain? The nervous system? It's been a problem, but also an attempted solution for psychologists of memory, since the earliest of inquiries. Physiological psychologists, those investigators of the physical representation of psychological events (experiences, memories, feelings, thoughts), had to make the assumption that for every mental event—learning a new name, for example—there must be a corresponding physiological one. In other words, something different must be present in the brain or at least the physical system once something new is entered into experience. If I just learned the name of

Milton Erickson for example, and you ask me who is the therapist who put people into trances and I answer "Milton Erickson," then it is clear something in my physiology must have "Milton Erickson" scratched on it. So you've now a right to ask, as the physiologists do, "Where is it?" This quest became known as the "search for the engram." Now that we've been overrun (taken over) by the computer and can use it as a model—not for nothing do we talk of its "memory" and refer to its usage capacity as so many megabytes—the model seems to have to work for humans too. Where is that bit or byte or engram called "Milton Erickson"?

The result of early experiments attempting to locate such a thing or what the physiology of learning might consist of (is it another physical change or perhaps a chemical one?) seemed to be anything but simple. A piece of learning turned out to be distributed throughout the organism. If you did experiments with flatworms, you discovered that it couldn't simply be in one place because after chopping an educated worm (one who'd learned something such as responding to light as a result of being reinforced for emerging from beneath the rock) into two, both of them responded to light. And when, after World War I, wounded soldiers had lost parts of their functioning because of brain damage, injuries which in earlier centuries would have proven fatal, they too illustrated regeneration and multiplicity of function. Capacities or functions thought to be localized could be taken over by other parts. So the question "Where is it?" seemed to be answered by "It's in many places."

Training, therefore, is not simply a matter of cardiovascular or oxidation or cellular or muscle change, although we know a bit about these and can be somewhat glib about their role. We can actually find that the mind, not just the brain, has the capacity which yields the change. One appeal of those monster or, more recently, "Jurassic Park" movies is our fascinating discovery that those creatures or robots are not simply acting on instinct, that they can "think," the most human character-istic of all. Even dinosaurs are not limited or simply pro-grammed by their neurons. Is it not also true of the machines? Was that not the nature of Poole and Bowman's fear of HAL in *2001*? Can we still say, when Deep Blue gives the world-champion chess masters pause, that it is obviously "only" a machine, only as good as its programmers? Isn't the question now not whether these machines think, but can we? That is, hasn't our thinking evolved and become more productive than that of even these highly developed machines? We are trained, yes, but can't we exceed our training?

My friend's daughter, an amateur runner who participates in triathlons and beats many professionals, does report that she hears her mind telling her she's in pain and must stop, but she "knows" that it's nonsense, just an excuse, something not to listen to, just a temptation, and forges on ahead. Her mind seems to be telling her mind to go away. So where is the "she" that is ignoring the other physical "she," except somewhere in the human or superhuman capacity to transcend our very lim-ited, even programmed, physiology?

Memory is of great interest beyond the physical, though again we're often tempted, particularly in the computer age, to think of it as "nothing but" the substratum.[72] When the computer "outputs" what's in its memory, it's the same bit or information resulting from the same bit that went in or that was programmed. Yes, I can produce these words again the same way, once I store them "into memory." That is, the com-puter's. But in human experience what is remembered is quite different from what was experienced. Memory recon-structs and, you might say, creates the past. According to one early researcher in the field, "Suppose I am making a stroke

---

72 It's of interest that systems of psychology can be separated into schools of "nothing but" (e.g., Behaviorism) and "something more" (e.g., Gestalt Psychology).

(in) tennis. I must relate new experiences to old ones ... I never really repeat something old."[73] Some may quarrel with this, shuddering as they remember their last frost or embarrassing tennis stroke with the same passion or bitterness or angst they felt originally, but I think we get the idea. And this is why, I'm convinced, there have been so many individuals who said "No more, never again. I'm glad I ran that marathon, but that's it, I'll never go through that training and rigor and pain again," then changed their minds and did another and another and another. Because what they remember is not the event or certainly not the total event. They remember as, the song says, the good times. Not the punishing hills and wet socks and frozen toes, but the faces of their loved ones at the finish line, a smiling photograph frozen into memory. Not the growls or frowns of their roommates or spouses or children or parents as they went out yet again to do nothing but run—and couldn't even take out the garbage, much less remember to pick up bread and milk—but the screams of joy and appreciation as they turned onto Fourth Avenue in Brooklyn, or onto East Side Drive at 90th Street, and all along the rest of the way until that last uphill climb 400 yards before the finish. Not the anxiety and lost sleep and nausea and other gastrointestinal problems, and pulled and strained and sprained and inflamed muscles and joints that accompanied so much of the training ordeal, but the glow of satisfaction at the end and the genuine congratulations that persisted for weeks and months, from old and new friends, from mere acquaintances who just heard what they'd done and reminded them that it was a real accomplishment.

If I haven't yet told you, I'm an exception, thank you. No mind change on the horizon, I've done mine. One, that's it.

---

73 F. Bartlett. *Remembering: A Study in Experimental and Social Psychology.* Cambridge, UK: Cambridge Univ. Press; 1967 (pp. 201–202).

If it's a trick of memory, the magic works and perhaps helps us get through quite a bit of our lives. It's why the funeral oration is not just a hypocritical display of the highlights of a person's life, but also is true: It's what we remember for the most part. It's why we congratulate those spouses celebrating their 50th anniversary. They too seem only, and not just publicly but also in their truest of hearts, to be remembering the good parts.

Memory, says Steinbeck somewhere, acts like a damp brush on a watercolor painting. The sharp edges disappear, the "ache" goes out of it, and out of the separate, distinct hues, a grayish, uniform pastiche emerges. There are other functions and characteristics of memory that Gestalt psychologists have taught us, and these too support this quality, dare we say it, of distortion. But it's distortion along understandable and predictable lines. In fact, these lines are a useful metaphor for conceiving of how memory works, and refer to principles of perception as well. One of the organizing principles, as they called them, was closure, the tendency to complete a figure that is incomplete. The most common example is that of a circle with a gap in its circumference. What do we see, they ask? And we answer, not an arc, but a circle with a hole in it, an indication that, perceptually, we're closing the circle—not distorting it, just completing it. We can't help noting that these days the term has become part of our everyday vocabulary, as when we seek to experience "closure" for events that are not quite complete. Even when it's clear that victims' disappearing, as after a boating accident or the events of September 11th, means they've died, we need to find the body or some remnant of it before we can properly grieve. And one often finds in therapy that when unresolved issues with the deceased stay unresolved, the griever cannot fully move on, for she has yet to close the chapter or the book. That person mentioned earlier in discussing "denial," whose father's terminal sickness had been kept from her, never had a chance to accept it or to say goodbye properly. So she dreamt of him for years, a display of the effort of the unconscious to finish some process.

Incomplete tasks, as discovered decades ago by Bluma Zeigarnik, are recalled more than completed ones—in fact, almost twice as readily, according to her studies.[74] This result was originally referred to as the "Berlin waiter effect," the result of Zeigarnik noticing in cafés that waiters could precisely retain for a few hours prodigious amounts of material (what people ordered) without writing anything down. But a minute after the customers had paid, they could not. The job was finished, there was no need to remember. And even if you offered them an incentive, they couldn't remember. The need for customers to be billed had kept the memory as well as the accounting books open.

Closure is a special case of what was called *Pragnanz*, the tendency to make a figure "better": more complete, more symmetrical, more balanced.[75] Though the model was from perception, it holds as well for memory. So if presented with a three-sided figure with a curved side and a dotted side and a squiggly side, we still see the triangle—provided the curves, dots and squiggles aren't overwhelming—and mentally or perceptually get rid of the "imperfections." And our memory improves on those imperfections as well. Did we stumble in our races? Did we stop before continuing? Did we get there late on that miserable Sunday by taking the most circuitous of routes? Not according to the recollection of many, which straightens things out and recalls the course as more or less direct and the result outstanding, regardless of the process.

---

74 K. Lewin and B. Zeigarnik. *Psychol. Forsch:* 9; 1927. Cited in: W. Kohler. *Dynamics in Psychology*. New York: Washington Square Press; 1962 (p. 52).

75 The literal meaning of "pregnant" is not the most common one; it refers to the capability of yielding something fruitful, meaningful, a potential yet to be discovered, as a "pregnant" pause or an idea's being "pregnant" with possibilities. E. Heidbreder. *Seven Psychologies*. New York: Appleton–Century–Croft; 1970 (p. 349).

Finally, this principle is also consistent with another that is referred to as "continuance" or, originally, "good continuation." If we follow a line passing through a square, we don't see a series of interrupted partial figures; we see a square with a curved line going through it. If we tell a "good" story, it follows along simple, predictable lines. It may have its detours, but those are not haphazard like static on the screen, they're patterned. So our memories follow those simple lines as well. Yes, they get distorted. Remember that game of "telephone" in which a whispered story in one ear emerges quite differently after a dozen retellings? But the story doesn't get infinitely more complex. It gets reduced. The sharp edges or "aches" go out of it.

So our remembrances of races, training runs, marathons, and even practices past are not quite as they occurred. Whether a defense or a trick or an organizing principle, such a distortion may not be a bad thing, as it provides an incentive to move on to a different course or, for those who choose, to do it all over again. We may capture more moments when we're given to reflection and even to writing books on the subject, as we may do well to remember the complexity of the lives of our deceased friends when we give ourselves the luxury and time, but not if we're getting up to run again. So memory's distortions, like history's, enable us to profit a bit from the past, but also to surpass its limitations.

14

The Final Run-Through—
Epilogue

$\mathbf{N}$ow that it's over, I'm reminded of those last few yards of the race. As I mentioned at the outset, aside from inquiring whether my legs had "turned yet to noodles," Vicki's most pressing question, even as I ran by her side for part of those last five miles, was "Is it fun yet?" I looked at her in disbelief, and with a wry smile responded, "Not yet." Which was quite the truth.

Not until the last 400 yards, when I soared up the last modest incline past the cheering crowd, was I able finally to relax a bit. "Hey," said one of my sons when he saw the finishing picture, "Your hands were up. I never saw you do that." No, I was always too busy stretching my hands forward at all finish lines (of my modest dozen or so races these last two years), like a sprinter leaning for the tape, trying to shave a tenth of a second off his time. Here I was congratulating myself and for a moment finding it hard to admit, for some reason, that it was almost fun. Although even if it wasn't, what of it? It was worth it. Not everything has to be fun. I've spoken earlier of the seduction of "fun," like the quick fix, not giving the lasting sense of well-being that results from something longer, from something into which one has had to put considerable work.

But there were also those mixed feelings at the finish line. Some of it was exhilarating, most of it was fatiguing, but it felt like more was needed. After so long a buildup, one step was not going to finish it. I needed to think about it. Perhaps I needed to write about it. Perhaps I needed to improve on it. This was good, but not with a capital "G," not the Gospel. The Torah in Judaism is endlessly interpreted because even texts that are gone over for centuries always reveal something new. There is always *d'var echeer,* another word; indeed, we are told that there are in the Torah *shevayeem,* seventy interpretations, seventy faces, seventy perspectives on the event. Deena Kastor, moving in rhythm and balanced by *kaizen* (referred to in Chapter Four), is also provided the passion to continue, constantly to strive, despite knowing you won't reach the pinnacle because someone else will always surpass your accomplishment. Is this why we're never satisfied? Always driven? Meaning, of course, we're always driving ourselves?

And dare I say, hearing my own quasireligious overtones, I learned that God indeed is in the details? Patients are always quasiapologetically excusing their concerns, prefacing their complaint or observation with, "Oh, it's not a big thing ... but ..." God is in the slight remark that those in-laws made. ("Oh, you made this yourself?") Or the passing "generous" remark that your ex made when you offered to spare him some trouble. ("Oh, are you sure you'll have time? I know how busy you are.") Or in the absence of any remark I made to a patient's polite greeting in the waiting room, allowing a wealth of conjectures to grow. Or in the toenails. Their structure, their current condition, their deformities, ever so slight, take oh-so-much time. An extra five minutes to get on those socks, once the toenails are dislodged and hanging at precarious ninety-degree angles from their normal positions and you don't dare yet wrench them from their roots, for who knows what trouble lurks beneath? Hey macho guy, we might hear from you what was always thought to be the classic Princess excuse for needing more time: "I've cracked a nail." And remember those bathroom necessities made all the more urgent under the influence of exercise, particularly as you approach the starting line? It's a whole different ballgame when your main concern in the dugout is over plumbing.

I mentioned in the section on metaphor how my perception of time has changed, as has that of distance. (There's a transit strike? I can't get to Brooklyn? Guess again. Mapquest tells me it's only 15.1 miles. I can run it. I've done 26.2!) As I was carefully following the running schedule, the months before the marathon became a distinct blur and passed very quickly. I couldn't believe that eight weeks had gone by since I attended that convention in Washington or did the Manhattan half-marathon, but suddenly it was October, three weeks before the big event. Paying such attention to the small amount of time seemed to alter perception of the large. I was like the reverse of the prisoner in solitary confinement, who thinks years have gone by when he's been in isolation for a couple of weeks. So much attention to minutes, even seconds, in calculating my pace; so much worry about the day-to-day progress and hoping, if not for a personal best, at least some discernible minute sign that I was progressing; so much exhilaration in breaking my own per-mile pace in a 5K race; so much anxiety over how many minutes I could afford to run and not be late for a patient. I squeezed so much out of each quarter-hour that never again can I afford to say, "Sorry, I don't have the time." Or if I do, there will be no guilt because now I have a very clear meaning of what it means.

Now that it's over, moreover, I have a curious dilemma, one that may very well be unique. One of the things running taught me was the importance of planning and executing (as the football commentators say about the team's efforts) the plan. Go the extra mile. Go the first mile. Get out the door, even, especially, when the wind and other appointments are howling in your face.

And this is absolutely important when it comes to writing. The writing teachers have often advocated it, "daily writing," sitting down at the keyboard on schedule even if you have to strap yourself into your chair, because it's always hard to get started. There is intermittent noise, perpetual hunger, and all the self-imposed tasks that can't be neglected, even if you're not a talk-show host. So though I need to go out there, snow and all, and get some exercise, I can't quite, not unless I go the extra page. Running has indeed taught me to go the extra mile, or at least a few more yards, with everything else, sometimes even at the expense of running.

And while it may be obvious, it's also taught me about procrastination, which is not just the great tendency to put something off, but to put it off once it's begun. I spoke of this earlier, it being the result of irrational beliefs, from the vantage point of the cognitive therapist, but it can also stem from not wanting to lose what you have at the moment. (The cognitive therapist might ask, "Would it be terrible if you did?") Shall I make it to the bank now for a fifteen-minute transaction and risk losing my computer time at the library or shopping time or tennis time? Yes, because later it will be harder, you'll have to recapture even for that simple transaction the calculations or the deposit slips. So when you get there, only your withdrawal tendencies (!) may be paramount. Do it, says Nike, and they're right. Do it early. Do it at 6:00 a.m.

But here's another irony. If you don't finish it, it pays to have started it nevertheless, because you're on your way. If you really had to finish one task before doing another, you might end up doing just that, finishing but one. When I'm running (operating) on schedule, I'm moving smoothly, without a hitch, without breaking stride. And if I stop, even to tie a shoelace or take a bathroom break, I've lost something. But—and here's the rub—remembering the Zeigarnik effect, the interruption also gives me the incentive to finish the task.

Let's rub further. If running has taught me I can't always be running when I want to, I've also learned that when my mind runs (crashes) into a wall, one of the better places to replenish it is from my own runs. In short, from running I learn to schedule things, which means I can't run because I've scheduled writing about running, which means I have to run to get ideas about running about which to write.

And that may explain something of the contradiction we see in so much of sport analyses, even the modest ones, with respect to running. My most immediate example is this remarkable 2005 New York Marathon, the one of which I now realize I was privileged to be a part. Since I've played it over and over, let's, as Warner Wolf would say, go back to the videotape.

The announcement was made at some point that "male testosterone can be a problem." The observation was voiced to point out the poor strategy that Hendrik Ramaala, last year's winner, was using at the 18-mile point of the race, when he decided to spurt ahead a few times rather than stay with the pack of four that had been together for most of the race. Meb Keflezighi, the American by way of Eritrea, the surprise silver medalist at the previous year's Olympics and surprise second-place finisher to Ramaala the year before, was "playing it smart," not being tempted to keep up.

The result was that Ramaala came in second by the narrowest of margins, 0.31 seconds, and Keflezighi was 26 seconds back in third. This is not a huge difference, but I cite it as testimony to how often commentators are wrong because the theory is wrong, or because it has an equal chance of being right or wrong (theoretically). To establish its truth, one would have to compare races where these spurts have and have not occurred, whether indeed it's a function of testosterone arrogance or a shrewd move or both or neither. Katherine Switzer, who was doing commentary on the women's race, called the winner, the underdog Latvian Jelena Prokopcuka, a good four or five miles before the end because she noted correctly that the Kenyan Susan Chepkemie was, though side by side with the Latvian for the last six miles, beginning to weave a bit. Also noted was how Paul Tergat, the eventual winner, was the "alpha male" from the start, the head of the pack that all others had to heed. But as soon as they indicated that looking around at the other runners (again, Ramaala's tendency) was a poor strategy, they quickly added, "Unless it's to see what the others are up to."

It would be nice to hear admitted that too often, we just don't know. The sports media experts find that particularly hard to do. While psychology is about trying to understand and predict what humans do, behavior, you may have noted, is quite complex and seemingly contradictory unless we find the correct analysis to separate the seeming contradictions. Therapy, in a way, often affords this opportunity. A person is early and then late. The same person. But a different motive. So the germane variable, to get technical, is not what she does with time, but what she wants to do. Others are a distraction but also a source of motivation. And motivation, as we've indicated, while fundamental, is complex. Is it "achievement" or is it "competition"? You need to know your subjects.

And with sports teams as well as individuals, the theory is often weak and the predictions wrong, if they're even testable. We can predict that a horse will run faster when others are around it, or even which candidate (of two or three) will likely win the gubernatorial race based on our preliminary or exit polls, or even how long we're likely to live or which kid will

The Final Run-Through—Epilogue   201

have a good chance of success in college, but not whether Seattle will beat Pittsburgh or the point spread in the Super Bowl. A lot, so I hear, depends on the referees. And that is also what keeps the bookmakers in business.

When the relationship is simple or when there's a gross comparison—Bloomberg's up 20 percent in the polls—we can be on target with our predictions. But if you listen closely to most of the analysts, nothing is being said because everything is being said. Looking around is a good thing because the top runners look for signs of weakness, like Chepkemei vomiting or Keflezighi wobbling—except when it's a bad thing.

Sometimes it's mere incomprehensibility that we hear, masquerading as astute observation. "The African runners believe First Avenue is where you win the race, and the Europeans that it's where you lose."[76] Are those different? Does one not imply the other? I guess if you mean, as Tiger Woods does when he talks about golf, or as should be obvious from any "elimination" tournament like tennis, that you can only lose in the first round and not win, then it makes sense. By rule, you're eliminated if you don't make the cut or don't win your first-round match. To win the tournament, however, you have to be in it to the very end. But if you mean that when you get a big lead, then that's where you've won it, then *io ipso,* as night follows day, that's also where someone else has lost it. So if runner X has opened up that insurmountable lead at mile 16 and there's no catching him, (except maybe if he makes a wrong turn à la German Silva, who still held on to win by two seconds) then that's where runner Y—and Z and A and B— have lost it, since they are too far behind.

We can add to this allegation of analysis-incompetence the all-too-familiar cop-out of explaining the winner by suggesting he's the one "who came to run." As if motivation were all there was to it. Yes, it's hard to believe those four in the front of the

---

76 Or so said the on-air commentator.

pack, or those 18 in the front of the pack, or even those 37,000 behind them (including, most of all, me; you think running for five hours is a walk in the park?) did not come to run. But even if we don't take it so literally, what, if anything, is being said? That we can't tell who's going to win. So we jump into "who wants it more," who was really "hungry enough for victory," and with Philosophy 101 circular illogical reasoning, conclude that whoever won wanted it more because if you don't want it more, you don't win. You don't think that Ramaala's falling at the tape or Chepkemei throwing up along the route meant they were hungry enough? They were so hungry, they fainted or got indigestion.

Kathryn Switzer implied this sad, confusing conclusion once again when she volunteered the thought that things are just so hard when your mind tells your body to do something but the body just doesn't respond. Remember my friend's daughter rejecting her mind's counsel? If Switzer is right, so much for the mental side of things, so much for telling us the second half of the marathon or the last six miles are a matter of heart and mind. So much for sexual therapy. So much for any kind of therapy.

On my first run in the last two weeks of training, the time I'd been looking forward to as "tapering," the weather was awful, blustery and rainy. But I decided I had to get in my first of a series of five-milers and with a moderate schedule of appointments, I had only one possible time slot. The rain had its own schedule. Within minutes, my shorts were falling down under the sweatpants I hadn't worn in months and I had to stop to adjust. By then the downpour was so heavy and the wind so bad that I could hardly move against it. For the first time in my brief running career, I decided I couldn't reach my original goal, that it was ridiculous under these conditions, and that I would settle for doing two miles, maybe three. I had good reason. I reminded myself of the virtue of flexibility. I could always find room later in the week for what I missed. But then, when I turned around and felt less wind as an obstacle, I decided to see if I could get four. So I kept going. And the wind returned. But now it was a little less severe. And then I discovered I had already, somewhere in the recesses of my consciousness, made up my mind to go for the original five. By now I'd be a bit late for the first appointment, but it wasn't critical. I could have managed with a compromise, but I shocked myself by pushing, realizing that pushing is what this damned thing called running, this damned thing called life, was perhaps all about. And as I did it, I recalled the sanitation worker seven months earlier in March, clearing some of the snow and ice, remarking as I went by, "Now there's a jogger," and how pleased I was to hear it. Running may not be the most significant thing I've done in my life, but it certainly has been one of the more arduous.

Of even greater psychological interest to me was that despite all the advice, much of which I was able to follow in training, nobody else's experience counted so much as my own. I thought for sure, especially when it came down to those last few miles, that if I ever got there I'd use Huckabee's trick about thinking of each mile as representative of a person I knew and wouldn't want to disappoint. Mile 19 for Aunt Goldie. Mile 20 for Grandpa Moshe. Not only didn't I do it, it never occurred to me. I had prepared myself to follow Matthew's advice of concentrating on the peoples' feet in front of me as a last resort if it became excruciating, but I not only didn't need it, I also forgot completely about it. I thought I'd get through some of the worst parts—those five hilly bridges, that last Fifth Avenue or Central Park South gradual incline—by doing some of my distracting mantras, counting days, numbers, exercise machines, women, childhood friends, enemies, accounts payable, but I never did. I don't know if it even occurred to me.

Despite my cute early list of all the reasons I wasn't suited for this enterprise, I've come to realize despite myself that I may not be so unsuited as I thought. Hard as it is for me to admit, I may actually be able, finally, to generate a few reasons why running fits:

1) I'm organized. I get everything in. Even when I'm in Montreal or Washington, I run. I do it outside or get into gyms somehow. I bring along suitable clothes just in case.

2) I persevere. Not till the woman definitely doesn't call back do I give up. If Medicaid refuses, "pends," I go after them, even when they've impossibly screwed up the birth dates. Patients who don't pay hear from me. Again and again, if need be. If I can't get on the Chinese-run (operated) bus from Washington because it's overbooked, I wait to see if there'll be any no-shows rather than agree to take the next one two hours later. And when the computer freezes or won't wake up or can't straighten out because of "disk error" or "disk full" or "slipped disk," or erases all documents beginning with "D" or substitutes one punctuation mark or file for another without so much as announcing in the playbill that "Tonight, the part of 'Personality' will be played by 'Perception,'" I do not hesitate in loudly cursing the technological gods, yet still, even if not at full stride, roll the boulder up the Sisyphean hill once more.

3) I'm fast. When traversing the city, I plan each block so as not to hit a light.

4) I'm competitive. You think this activity (okay, sport) is all about one's own inner drummer? Now when I see those well-dressed, unsweating East Side lasses coming home from their mile or two in the park, I think, "Ahh, you call yourself runners, eh?" How quickly we move up in class and become a snob; but to the driven, how much of a motivator such ladder-climbing can be.

5) I'm narcissistic. I like to play tennis in the front court where people can watch. George Carlin recently admitted this showboating tendency as the source of his becoming a stand-up comedian. At age nine he was doing imitations so people would recognize him and approve. I too want everyone to see and applaud my accomplishments. I want them to say, "You're amazing," which is what some of them did. I've hung up the pictures the kids took en route all over the place. I was prepared to fail, but every ounce of my survival narcissism fought it. It got me through. How else could I look anyone in the face?

6) I'm resilient. I keep going. Everything's always going. Things could always be worse. That perhaps is a residue of the nomadic people from whom I come, leading me to ...

7) I'm Jewish. And it's not at all antithetical to running. We're always on the march. Many oppressed people are. And when one rabbi dies, another takes his place. Or so the myth goes.

8) I'm Jewish. When the rabbi was asked about his *kevanah,* the intensity of his prayer, and how he kept it up all the time, he admitted he didn't. But, he added, one of the consequences of not doing it all the time is that you realize you're practicing for when you can. So once again, the run isn't good all the time, but it doesn't have to be. Wait. It will come. Before the Messiah, I hope.

9) I'm Jewish. When I first got on the treadmill and was told where to stand and finally figured out which direction to face, it didn't seem that strange. Standing in one place, with a slight sway, getting nowhere, was all too familiar. It was like *davening* (just in case your ancestors come from a different part of the world than mine, this is the Yiddish term for "praying," often while rocking back and forth).

10) I'm a good sport. I like to win, but I don't throw victory in the face of my opponents, even when they're talkative,

score-forgetting, lousy line-callers in tennis. I know victory is transient, even if I can never remember or fully understand that Kipling quote about those two imposters. And I know how to lose. I've had plenty of practice.

Index

2001 (movie), 189

A

achievement motivation, 145, 149, 150, 153
addictions, 16, 101–3
Adler, Alfred, 91
Agassi, Andre, 42, 68, 127n
aging, 7, 9, 27, 73, 75
Allen, Woody, 64
anger, 67–69
anxiety, 66
Apollo, 103; *see also* Dionysius
apperceptive mass, phenomenon of the, 181
Aristotelian causes, relationship of sport explanations to, 35
associators, 86, 87, 89, 154–55; *see also* dissociators
athletic identity, 153

B

Bartlett, Frederick C., 190n
basketball, 38
"Berlin waiter effect," 192
bipolar disorder, 93, 111, 121
Blake, James, 42, 127–28, 127n
Blink, see Gladwell, Malcolm
Borg, Bjorn, *see* tennis and emotions
Buber, Martin, 6
Byron, Lord (George), 24

C

caffeine, 4, 26
Carlin, George, 60, 205
cell phones, 3, 37, 85, 87

Central Park, 10, 12, 45, 62, 68, 76, 86, 114, 125, 164, 170, 203
Central Park Jogger, 45, 106, 121; *see also* Meili, Trisha
Chanukah, 181
Chepkemei, Susan, 155, 163, 200, 202
chess, 57
children as teachers, 8–9, 10–14
closure, 191–92
cognitive dissonance, 181–82
competition as motive, 149, 150, 153
confidence, 19
counterphobic behavior, 124
Crystal, Billy, 64
Csikszentmihalyi, Mihaly, 113, 173, 179

D

dating services, 112
denial, 127–28
depression, 107–9, 121
determinism, 117–18
deviances, fashionable, 113n
Dionysius, 103; *see also* Apollo
dissociators, 86, 88, 90, 154; *see also* associators
distance, perspective on, 71–72, 197
DSM, 81, 93

E

ectomorphs, 11
eidetic imagery, 168
Ellis, Albert, 157, 158
emotions, role of, 66–69
Erickson, Milton, 58–59, 178–79

Bibliography

Allport, Gordon. *Becoming: Basic Considerations for a Psychology of Personality.* New Haven, CT: Yale U. Press, 1955.

Brown, Roger. *Social Psychology.* New York: Free Press, 1986.

Burfoot, Amby (Ed.), *Runners' World Complete Book of Running: Everything You Need to Know to Run for Fun, Fitness, and Competition.* Emmaus, PA: Rodale Press, 1997.
— *The Principles of Running: Practical Lessons from my First 100,000 Miles.* Emmaus, PA: Rodale Press, 1999.
— *The Runner's Guide to the Meaning of Life.* Emmaus, PA: Rodale Press, 2000.

Csikszentmihalyi, Mihaly. *Flow: The Psychology of Optimal Experience.* New York: Harper Collins, 1990.

Drenth, Tere. *Marathon Training for Dummies.* New York: Wiley, 2003.

Fischer, Helen. *The Anatomy of Love.* New York: W.W. Norton, 1992.

Freud, Sigmund. *A General Introduction to Psychoanalysis* (transl. Joan Riviere). New York: Washington Square Press, 1962.
— *Civilization and its Discontents* (transl. James Strachey). New York: W.W. Norton, 1962.
— *New Introductory Lectures on Psychoanalysis* (transl. James Strachey). New York: W.W. Norton, 1965.

Galloway, Jeff. *Training Journal.* Atlanta, GA: Phidippides, 1998.
— *Marathon.* Atlanta, GA: Phidippides, 2000.

Gallwey, W. Timothy. *The Inner Game of Tennis.* New York: Random House, 1974.

Gazzaniga, Michael and Todd Heatherton. *Psychological Science: Mind, Brain and Behavior.* New York: W.W. Norton, 2003.

Gladwell, Malcolm. *Blink: The Power of Thinking Without Thinking.* New York: Little, Brown and Co., 2005.

Glover, Bob, Jack Shepherd & Shelly-Lynn Florence Glover. *The Runner's Handbook.* New York: Penguin, 1996.

Hall, Edward. *The Hidden Dimension.* Garden City, NY: Doubleday, 1966.
— *The Silent Language.* Greenwich, CT: Fawcett, 1959.

Heibreder, Edna. *Seven Psychologies.* New York: Appleton-Century-Crofts, 1933.

Hendrick, Clyde. *Group Processes and Intergroup Relations.* Newbury Park, CA: Sage, 1987.

Higdon, Hal. *Masters Running: A Guide to Training and Staying Fit after 40.* Emmaus, PA: Rodale, 2005.

Horney, Karen. *The Neurotic Personality of Our Times.* New York: W.W. Norton, 1937.

Huckabee, Mike. *Stop Digging Your Grave with a Knife and Fork: A 12-Step Program to Begin a Healthy Lifestyle.* New York: Center Street, 2005.

Jung, Carl. *Psychological Types.* Princeton, NJ: Princeton U. Press, 1971. ˙

Kislevitz, Gail. *First Marathons: Personal Encounters with the 26.2-Mile Monster.* Halcottsville, New York: Breakaway Books, 1999.

Laing, Ronald D. *Politics of the Family.* New York: Pantheon, 1971.

LeUnes, Arnold and Jack Nation. *Sport Psychology* (3rd Ed.) Pacific Grove, CA: Wadsworth, 2002.

Liberman, Art. *The Everything Running Book: From Circling the Block to Completing a Marathon, Tricks and Tips to Make You a Better Runner.* Avon, MA: Adams Media Corporation, 2002.

Lindzey, Gardner and Elliot Aronson (Eds.) *The Handbook of Social Psychology.* Reading, MA: Addison-Wesley, 1968.

Lynch, Jerry and Warren Scott. *Running Within.* Champaign, IL: Human Kinetics, 1999.

Maccoby, Eleanor & Carol Jacklin. *The Psychology of Sex Differences.* Stanford, CA: Stanford U. Press, 1974.

Maharam, Lewis. *Maharam's Curve: The Exercise High-How to Get It, How to Keep It.* New York: W. W. Norton, 1992.

Maslow, Abraham. *Toward a Psychology of Being.* Princeton, NJ: Van Nostrand, 1968.

May, Rollo. *Love and Will.* New York: W. W. Norton, 1969.

Meili, Trisha. *I Am the Central Park Jogger: A Story of Hope and Possibility.* New York: Scribner, 2003.

Mullahy, Patrick. *Oedipus, Myth and Complex.* New York: Grove Press, 1948.

Rodgers, Bill and Douglas Scott. *The Complete Idiot's Guide to Running* (2nd Ed.). Indianapolis, IN: Alpha, 1998.

Rogers, Carl. *On Becoming a Person.* Boston, MA: Houghton-Mifflin, 1961.

Rosenthal, Robert. *Pygmalion in the Classroom.* New York: Holt, Rinehart and Winston, 1981.

Sartre, Jean-Paul. *No Exit + Three Other Plays.* New York: Vintage, 1973.

Seligman, Martin. *Helplessness: On Depression, Development and Death.* San Francisco, CA: W. H. Freeman, 1975.

Simmel, Edward. *Social Facilitation and Imitative Behavior* (Outcome of the 1967 Miami University Symposium on Social Behavior). Boston, MA: Allyn and Bacon, 1968.

Sulloway, Frank. *Born to Rebel.* New York: Vintage, 1997.

Van Raalte, Judy & Britton Brewer. *Exploring Sport and Exercise Psychology.* Washington, D.C.: APA, 1996.

Webb, Tamilee. *Workouts for Dummies.* New York: Hungry Minds, 1998.

Westen, Drew. *Psychology: Brain, Behavior and Culture.* Cambridge, MA: Cambridge U. Press, 1985.

Zeig, Jeffrey. *A Teaching Seminar with Milton H. Erickson* (Annual Progress in Child Psychiatry and Child Development). Philadelphia, PA: Brunner/Mazel, 1980.